FREE Test Taking Tips DVD Offer

To help us better serve you, we have developed a Test Taking Tips DVD that we would like to give you for FREE. **This DVD covers world-class test taking tips that you can use to be even more successful when you are taking your test.**

All that we ask is that you email us your feedback about your study guide. Please let us know what you thought about it – whether that is good, bad or indifferent.

To get your **FREE Test Taking Tips DVD**, email freedvd@studyguideteam.com with "FREE DVD" in the subject line and the following information in the body of the email:

     a. The title of your study guide.

     b. Your product rating on a scale of 1-5, with 5 being the highest rating.

     c. Your feedback about the study guide. What did you think of it?

     d. Your full name and shipping address to send your free DVD.

If you have any questions or concerns, please don't hesitate to contact us at freedvd@studyguideteam.com.

Thanks again!

SAT English Practice
SAT Grammar Workbook Tutor
with 3 Practice Tests
[2nd Edition Prep]

TPB Publishing

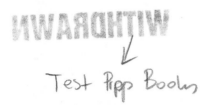

WITHDRAWN
Test Prep Books

Interested in buying more than 10 copies of our product? Contact us about bulk discounts:
bulkorders@studyguideteam.com

ISBN 13: 9781628458152
ISBN 10: 1628458151

Table of Contents

Quick Overview

As you draw closer to taking your exam, effective preparation becomes more and more important. Thankfully, you have this study guide to help you get ready. Use this guide to help keep your studying on track and refer to it often.

This study guide contains several key sections that will help you be successful on your exam. The guide contains tips for what you should do the night before and the day of the test. Also included are test-taking tips. Knowing the right information is not always enough. Many well-prepared test takers struggle with exams. These tips will help equip you to accurately read, assess, and answer test questions.

A large part of the guide is devoted to showing you what content to expect on the exam and to helping you better understand that content. In this guide are practice test questions so that you can see how well you have grasped the content. Then, answer explanations are provided so that you can understand why you missed certain questions.

Don't try to cram the night before you take your exam. This is not a wise strategy for a few reasons. First, your retention of the information will be low. Your time would be better used by reviewing information you already know rather than trying to learn a lot of new information. Second, you will likely become stressed as you try to gain a large amount of knowledge in a short amount of time. Third, you will be depriving yourself of sleep. So be sure to go to bed at a reasonable time the night before. Being well-rested helps you focus and remain calm.

Be sure to eat a substantial breakfast the morning of the exam. If you are taking the exam in the afternoon, be sure to have a good lunch as well. Being hungry is distracting and can make it difficult to focus. You have hopefully spent lots of time preparing for the exam. Don't let an empty stomach get in the way of success!

When travelling to the testing center, leave earlier than needed. That way, you have a buffer in case you experience any delays. This will help you remain calm and will keep you from missing your appointment time at the testing center.

Be sure to pace yourself during the exam. Don't try to rush through the exam. There is no need to risk performing poorly on the exam just so you can leave the testing center early. Allow yourself to use all of the allotted time if needed.

Remain positive while taking the exam even if you feel like you are performing poorly. Thinking about the content you should have mastered will not help you perform better on the exam.

Once the exam is complete, take some time to relax. Even if you feel that you need to take the exam again, you will be well served by some down time before you begin studying again. It's often easier to convince yourself to study if you know that it will come with a reward!

Test-Taking Strategies

1. Predicting the Answer

When you feel confident in your preparation for a multiple-choice test, try predicting the answer before reading the answer choices. This is especially useful on questions that test objective factual knowledge. By predicting the answer before reading the available choices, you eliminate the possibility that you will be distracted or led astray by an incorrect answer choice. You will feel more confident in your selection if you read the question, predict the answer, and then find your prediction among the answer choices. After using this strategy, be sure to still read all of the answer choices carefully and completely. If you feel unprepared, you should not attempt to predict the answers. This would be a waste of time and an opportunity for your mind to wander in the wrong direction.

2. Reading the Whole Question

Too often, test takers scan a multiple-choice question, recognize a few familiar words, and immediately jump to the answer choices. Test authors are aware of this common impatience, and they will sometimes prey upon it. For instance, a test author might subtly turn the question into a negative, or he or she might redirect the focus of the question right at the end. The only way to avoid falling into these traps is to read the entirety of the question carefully before reading the answer choices.

3. Looking for Wrong Answers

Long and complicated multiple-choice questions can be intimidating. One way to simplify a difficult multiple-choice question is to eliminate all of the answer choices that are clearly wrong. In most sets of answers, there will be at least one selection that can be dismissed right away. If the test is administered on paper, the test taker could draw a line through it to indicate that it may be ignored; otherwise, the test taker will have to perform this operation mentally or on scratch paper. In either case, once the obviously incorrect answers have been eliminated, the remaining choices may be considered. Sometimes identifying the clearly wrong answers will give the test taker some information about the correct answer. For instance, if one of the remaining answer choices is a direct opposite of one of the eliminated answer choices, it may well be the correct answer. The opposite of obviously wrong is obviously right! Of course, this is not always the case. Some answers are obviously incorrect simply because they are irrelevant to the question being asked. Still, identifying and eliminating some incorrect answer choices is a good way to simplify a multiple-choice question.

4. Don't Overanalyze

Anxious test takers often overanalyze questions. When you are nervous, your brain will often run wild, causing you to make associations and discover clues that don't actually exist. If you feel that this may be a problem for you, do whatever you can to slow down during the test. Try taking a deep breath or counting to ten. As you read and consider the question, restrict yourself to the particular words used by the author. Avoid thought tangents about what the author *really* meant, or what he or she was *trying* to say. The only things that matter on a multiple-choice test are the words that are actually in the question. You must avoid reading too much into a multiple-choice question, or supposing that the writer meant something other than what he or she wrote.

5. No Need for Panic

It is wise to learn as many strategies as possible before taking a multiple-choice test, but it is likely that you will come across a few questions for which you simply don't know the answer. In this situation, avoid panicking. Because most multiple-choice tests include dozens of questions, the relative value of a single wrong answer is small. As much as possible, you should compartmentalize each question on a multiple-choice test. In other words, you should not allow your feelings about one question to affect your success on the others. When you find a question that you either don't understand or don't know how to answer, just take a deep breath and do your best. Read the entire question slowly and carefully. Try rephrasing the question a couple of different ways. Then, read all of the answer choices carefully. After eliminating obviously wrong answers, make a selection and move on to the next question.

6. Confusing Answer Choices

When working on a difficult multiple-choice question, there may be a tendency to focus on the answer choices that are the easiest to understand. Many people, whether consciously or not, gravitate to the answer choices that require the least concentration, knowledge, and memory. This is a mistake. When you come across an answer choice that is confusing, you should give it extra attention. A question might be confusing because you do not know the subject matter to which it refers. If this is the case, don't eliminate the answer before you have affirmatively settled on another. When you come across an answer choice of this type, set it aside as you look at the remaining choices. If you can confidently assert that one of the other choices is correct, you can leave the confusing answer aside. Otherwise, you will need to take a moment to try to better understand the confusing answer choice. Rephrasing is one way to tease out the sense of a confusing answer choice.

7. Your First Instinct

Many people struggle with multiple-choice tests because they overthink the questions. If you have studied sufficiently for the test, you should be prepared to trust your first instinct once you have carefully and completely read the question and all of the answer choices. There is a great deal of research suggesting that the mind can come to the correct conclusion very quickly once it has obtained all of the relevant information. At times, it may seem to you as if your intuition is working faster even than your reasoning mind. This may in fact be true. The knowledge you obtain while studying may be retrieved from your subconscious before you have a chance to work out the associations that support it. Verify your instinct by working out the reasons that it should be trusted.

8. Key Words

Many test takers struggle with multiple-choice questions because they have poor reading comprehension skills. Quickly reading and understanding a multiple-choice question requires a mixture of skill and experience. To help with this, try jotting down a few key words and phrases on a piece of scrap paper. Doing this concentrates the process of reading and forces the mind to weigh the relative importance of the question's parts. In selecting words and phrases to write down, the test taker thinks about the question more deeply and carefully. This is especially true for multiple-choice questions that are preceded by a long prompt.

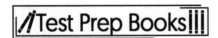

9. Subtle Negatives

One of the oldest tricks in the multiple-choice test writer's book is to subtly reverse the meaning of a question with a word like *not* or *except*. If you are not paying attention to each word in the question, you can easily be led astray by this trick. For instance, a common question format is, "Which of the following is...?" Obviously, if the question instead is, "Which of the following is not...?," then the answer will be quite different. Even worse, the test makers are aware of the potential for this mistake and will include one answer choice that would be correct if the question were not negated or reversed. A test taker who misses the reversal will find what he or she believes to be a correct answer and will be so confident that he or she will fail to reread the question and discover the original error. The only way to avoid this is to practice a wide variety of multiple-choice questions and to pay close attention to each and every word.

10. Reading Every Answer Choice

It may seem obvious, but you should always read every one of the answer choices! Too many test takers fall into the habit of scanning the question and assuming that they understand the question because they recognize a few key words. From there, they pick the first answer choice that answers the question they believe they have read. Test takers who read all of the answer choices might discover that one of the latter answer choices is actually *more* correct. Moreover, reading all of the answer choices can remind you of facts related to the question that can help you arrive at the correct answer. Sometimes, a misstatement or incorrect detail in one of the latter answer choices will trigger your memory of the subject and will enable you to find the right answer. Failing to read all of the answer choices is like not reading all of the items on a restaurant menu: you might miss out on the perfect choice.

11. Spot the Hedges

One of the keys to success on multiple-choice tests is paying close attention to every word. This is never truer than with words like almost, most, some, and sometimes. These words are called "hedges" because they indicate that a statement is not totally true or not true in every place and time. An absolute statement will contain no hedges, but in many subjects, the answers are not always straightforward or absolute. There are always exceptions to the rules in these subjects. For this reason, you should favor those multiple-choice questions that contain hedging language. The presence of qualifying words indicates that the author is taking special care with his or her words, which is certainly important when composing the right answer. After all, there are many ways to be wrong, but there is only one way to be right! For this reason, it is wise to avoid answers that are absolute when taking a multiple-choice test. An absolute answer is one that says things are either all one way or all another. They often include words like *every*, *always*, *best*, and *never*. If you are taking a multiple-choice test in a subject that doesn't lend itself to absolute answers, be on your guard if you see any of these words.

12. Long Answers

In many subject areas, the answers are not simple. As already mentioned, the right answer often requires hedges. Another common feature of the answers to a complex or subjective question are qualifying clauses, which are groups of words that subtly modify the meaning of the sentence. If the question or answer choice describes a rule to which there are exceptions or the subject matter is complicated, ambiguous, or confusing, the correct answer will require many words in order to be expressed clearly and accurately. In essence, you should not be deterred by answer choices that seem excessively long. Oftentimes, the author of the text will not be able to write the correct answer without

offering some qualifications and modifications. Your job is to read the answer choices thoroughly and completely and to select the one that most accurately and precisely answers the question.

13. Restating to Understand

Sometimes, a question on a multiple-choice test is difficult not because of what it asks but because of how it is written. If this is the case, restate the question or answer choice in different words. This process serves a couple of important purposes. First, it forces you to concentrate on the core of the question. In order to rephrase the question accurately, you have to understand it well. Rephrasing the question will concentrate your mind on the key words and ideas. Second, it will present the information to your mind in a fresh way. This process may trigger your memory and render some useful scrap of information picked up while studying.

14. True Statements

Sometimes an answer choice will be true in itself, but it does not answer the question. This is one of the main reasons why it is essential to read the question carefully and completely before proceeding to the answer choices. Too often, test takers skip ahead to the answer choices and look for true statements. Having found one of these, they are content to select it without reference to the question above. Obviously, this provides an easy way for test makers to play tricks. The savvy test taker will always read the entire question before turning to the answer choices. Then, having settled on a correct answer choice, he or she will refer to the original question and ensure that the selected answer is relevant. The mistake of choosing a correct-but-irrelevant answer choice is especially common on questions related to specific pieces of objective knowledge. A prepared test taker will have a wealth of factual knowledge at his or her disposal, and should not be careless in its application.

15. No Patterns

One of the more dangerous ideas that circulates about multiple-choice tests is that the correct answers tend to fall into patterns. These erroneous ideas range from a belief that B and C are the most common right answers, to the idea that an unprepared test-taker should answer "A-B-A-C-A-D-A-B-A." It cannot be emphasized enough that pattern-seeking of this type is exactly the WRONG way to approach a multiple-choice test. To begin with, it is highly unlikely that the test maker will plot the correct answers according to some predetermined pattern. The questions are scrambled and delivered in a random order. Furthermore, even if the test maker was following a pattern in the assignation of correct answers, there is no reason why the test taker would know which pattern he or she was using. Any attempt to discern a pattern in the answer choices is a waste of time and a distraction from the real work of taking the test. A test taker would be much better served by extra preparation before the test than by reliance on a pattern in the answers.

FREE DVD OFFER

Don't forget that doing well on your exam includes both understanding the test content and understanding how to use what you know to do well on the test. We offer a completely FREE Test Taking Tips DVD that covers world class test taking tips that you can use to be even more successful when you are taking your test.

All that we ask is that you email us your feedback about your study guide. To get your **FREE Test Taking Tips DVD**, email freedvd@studyguideteam.com with "FREE DVD" in the subject line and the following information in the body of the email:

- The title of your study guide.
- Your product rating on a scale of 1-5, with 5 being the highest rating.
- Your feedback about the study guide. What did you think of it?
- Your full name and shipping address to send your free DVD.

Introduction to the SAT

Function of the Test

The SAT is a standardized test taken by high school students across the United States and given internationally for college placement. It is designed to measure problem solving ability, communication, and understanding complex relationships. The SAT also serves as a qualifying measure to identify students for college scholarships, depending on the college being applied to. All colleges in the U.S. accept the SAT, and, in addition to admissions and scholarships, use SAT scores for course placement as well as academic counseling.

Most of the high school students who take the SAT are seniors. In 2016, the number of students who took the SAT was just under 1.7 million. It's important to note that since many updates have been implemented during the 2016 year, the data points cannot be compared to those in previous years. In 2014, 42.6 percent of students met the College Board's "college and career readiness" benchmark, and in 2015, 41.9 percent met this benchmark.

Test Administration

The SAT is offered on seven days throughout the year at schools throughout the United States. Internationally, the SAT is offered on five days throughout the year. There are thousands of testing centers worldwide. Test-takers can view the test centers in their area when they register for the test, or they can view testing locations at the College Board website, a not-for-profit that owns and publishes the SAT.

The SAT registration fee is $46, and the SAT with Essay registration fee is $60, although both of these have fee waivers available. Also note that students outside the U.S. may have to pay an extra processing fee. Additional fees include registering by phone, changing fee, late registration fee, or a waitlist fee. Test-takers may register four score reports for free up to nine days after the test. Any additional score reports cost $12, although fee waivers are available for this as well.

Test Format

The SAT gauges a student's proficiency in three areas: Reading, Mathematics, and Writing and Language. The reading portion of the SAT measures comprehension, requiring candidates to read multi-paragraph fiction and non-fiction segments including informational visuals, such as charts, tables and graphs, and answer questions based on this content. Fluency in problem solving, conceptual understanding of equations, and real-world applications are characteristics of the math test. The writing and language portion requires students to evaluate and edit writing and graphics to obtain an answer that correctly conveys the information given in the passage.

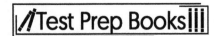

The SAT contains 154 multiple-choice questions, with each section comprising over 40 questions. A different length of time is given for each section, for a total of three hours, plus fifty minutes for the essay (optional).

Section	Time (In Minutes)	Number of Questions
Reading	65	52
Writing and Language	35	44
Mathematics	80	58
Essay (optional)	50 (optional)	1 (optional)
Total	**180**	**154 + optional essay**

Scoring

Scores for the new SAT are based on a scale from 400 to 1600. Scores range from 200 to 800 for Evidence-Based Reading and Writing, and 200 to 800 for Math. The optional essay is scored from 2 to 8. The SAT also no longer penalizes for incorrect answers. Therefore, a student's raw score is the number of correctly answered questions.

On the College Board website, there are indicators to determine what the benchmark scores are. The scores are divided up into green, yellow, or red. Green meets or exceeds the benchmark, and shows a 480 to 800 in Evidence-Based Reading and Writing, and a 530 to 800 in Math.

Recent/Future Developments

The SAT taken before March 2016 is different than the one administered currently. Currently, the essay is optional, and the time limit for the Reading, Writing, and Math sections has increased per section. The content features also vary, with the new test focusing on skills that research has identified as most important for college readiness and the meaning of words in extended context rather than emphasis on vocabulary. The score range has changed from 600–2400 to 400–1600. There has also been added subscore reporting, which provides insight to students and parents about the scores.

Parts of Speech

The English language has eight parts of speech, each serving a different grammatical function.

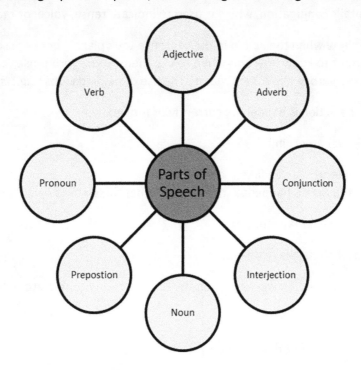

Verbs

A verb is the part of speech that describes an action, state of being, or occurrence.

A verb forms the main part of a predicate of a sentence. This means that the verb explains what the noun (which will be discussed shortly) is doing. A simple example is *time <u>flies</u>*. The verb *flies* explains what the action of the noun, *time*, is doing. This example is a *main* verb.

Helping (auxiliary) verbs are words like *have, do, be, can, may, should, must,* and *will.* "I *should* go to the store." Helping verbs assist main verbs in expressing tense, ability, possibility, permission, or obligation.

Particles are minor function words like *not, in, out, up,* or *down* that become part of the verb itself. "I might *not*."

Participles are words formed from verbs that are often used to modify a noun, noun phrase, verb, or verb phrase.

> The *running* teenager collided with the cyclist.

Participles can also create compound verb forms.

> He is *speaking*.

Verbs have five basic forms: the **base** form, the **-s** form, the **-ing** form, the **past** form, and the **past participle** form.

The past forms are either **regular** (*love/loved; hate/hated*) or **irregular** because they don't end by adding the common past tense suffix "-ed" (*go/went; fall/fell; set/set*).

Verb Forms

Shifting verb forms entails **conjugation,** which is used to indicate tense, voice, or mood.

Verb tense is used to show when the action in the sentence took place. There are several different verb tenses, and it is important to know how and when to use them. Some verb tenses can be achieved by changing the form of the verb, while others require the use of helping verbs (e.g., *is, was,* or *has*).

Present tense shows the action is happening currently or is ongoing:

> I walk to work every morning.

> She is stressed about the deadline.

Past tense shows that the action happened in the past or that the state of being is in the past:

> I walked to work yesterday morning.

> She was stressed about the deadline.

Future tense shows that the action will happen in the future or is a future state of being:

> I will walk to work tomorrow morning.

> She will be stressed about the deadline.

Present perfect tense shows action that began in the past, but continues into the present:

> I have walked to work all week.

> She has been stressed about the deadline.

Past perfect tense shows an action was finished before another took place:

> I had walked all week until I sprained my ankle.

> She had been stressed about the deadline until we talked about it.

Future perfect tense shows an action that will be completed at some point in the future:

> By the time the bus arrives, I will have walked to work already.

Voice

Verbs can be in the active or passive voice. When the subject completes the action, the verb is in **active voice.** When the subject receives the action of the sentence, the verb is in **passive voice.**

> Active: Jamie ate the ice cream.

> Passive: The ice cream was eaten by Jamie.

In active voice, the subject (*Jamie*) is the "do-er" of the action (*ate*). In passive voice, the subject *ice cream* receives the action of being eaten.

While passive voice can add variety to writing, active voice is the generally preferred sentence structure.

Nouns

A **noun** is a person, place, thing, or idea. All nouns fit into one of two types, common or proper.

A **common noun** is a word that identifies any of a class of people, places, or things. Examples include numbers, objects, animals, feelings, concepts, qualities, and actions. *A, an,* or *the* usually precedes the common noun. These parts of speech are called *articles*. Here are some examples of sentences using nouns preceded by articles.

A building is under construction.
The girl would like to move to *the* city.

A **proper noun** (also called a **proper name**) is used for the specific name of an individual person, place, or organization. The first letter in a proper noun is capitalized. "My name is *Mary*." "I work for *Walmart*."

Nouns sometimes serve as adjectives (which themselves describe nouns), such as "hockey player" and "state government."

- An **abstract noun** is an idea, state, or quality. It is something that can't be touched, such as happiness, courage, evil, or humor.

A **concrete noun** is something that can be experienced through the senses (touch, taste, hear, smell, see). Examples of concrete nouns are birds, skateboard, pie, and car.

A **collective noun** refers to a collection of people, places, or things that act as one. Examples of collective nouns are as follows: team, class, jury, family, audience, and flock.

Pronoun

A word used in place of a noun is known as a *pronoun*. Pronouns are words like *I, mine, hers,* and *us.*

Pronouns can be split into different classifications (see below) which make them easier to learn; however, it's not important to memorize the classifications.

- Personal pronouns: refer to people

- First person: we, I, our, mine

- Second person: you, yours

- Third person: he, them

- Possessive pronouns: demonstrate ownership (mine, his, hers, its, ours, theirs, yours)

- Interrogative pronouns: ask questions (what, which, who, whom, whose)

- Relative pronouns: include the five interrogative pronouns and others that are relative (whoever, whomever, that, when, where)

- Demonstrative pronouns: replace something specific (this, that, those, these)

- Reciprocal pronouns: indicate something was done or given in return (each other, one another)

- Indefinite pronouns: have a nonspecific status (anybody, whoever, someone, everybody, somebody)

Indefinite pronouns such as *anybody, whoever, someone, everybody*, and *somebody* command a singular verb form, but others such as *all, none,* and *some* could require a singular or plural verb form.

An *antecedent* is the noun to which a pronoun refers; it needs to be written or spoken before the pronoun is used. For many pronouns, antecedents are imperative for clarity. In particular, many of the personal, possessive, and demonstrative pronouns need antecedents. Otherwise, it would be unclear who or what someone is referring to when they use a pronoun like *he* or *this*.

Pronoun reference means that the pronoun should refer clearly to one, clear, unmistakable noun (the antecedent).

Pronoun-antecedent agreement refers to the need for the antecedent and the corresponding pronoun to agree in gender, person, and number. Here are some examples:

The *kidneys* (plural antecedent) are part of the urinary system. *They* (plural pronoun) serve several roles.

The kidneys are part of the *urinary system* (singular antecedent). *It* (singular pronoun) is also known as the renal system.

The subjective pronouns —*I, you, he/she/it, we, they,* and *who*—are the subjects of the sentence.

Example: *They* have a new house.

The objective pronouns—*me, you* (*singular*), *him/her, us, them,* and *whom*—are used when something is being done for or given to someone; they are objects of the action.

Example: The teacher has an apple for *us*.

The possessive pronouns—*mine, my, your, yours, his, hers, its, their, theirs, our,* and *ours*—are used to denote that something (or someone) belongs to someone (or something).

Example: It's *their* chocolate cake.

Even Better Example: It's *my* chocolate cake!

One of the greatest challenges and worst abuses of pronouns concerns *who* and *whom*. Just knowing the following rule can eliminate confusion. *Who* is a subjective-case pronoun used only as a subject or subject complement. *Whom* is only objective-case and, therefore, the object of the verb or preposition.

Who is going to the concert?

You are going to the concert with *whom*?

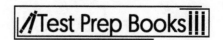

Hint: When using *who* or *whom*, think of whether someone would say *he* or *him*. If the answer is *he*, use *who*. If the answer is *him*, use *whom*. This trick is easy to remember because *he* and *who* both end in vowels, and *him* and *whom* both end in the letter *M*.

Adjective

Adjectives are words used to modify nouns and pronouns. They can be used alone or in a series and are used to further define or describe the nouns they modify.

> Mark made us a delicious, four-course meal.

The words *delicious* and *four-course* are adjectives that describe the kind of meal Mark made.

Articles are also considered adjectives because they help to describe nouns. Articles can be general or specific. The three articles in English are: a, an, and the.

Indefinite articles *(a, an)* are used to refer to nonspecific nouns. The article *a* proceeds words beginning with consonant sounds, and the article *an* proceeds words beginning with vowel sounds.

> A car drove by our house.

> An alligator was loose at the zoo.

> He has always wanted a ukulele. (The first *u* makes a *y* sound.)

Note that *a* and *an* should only proceed nonspecific nouns that are also singular. If a nonspecific noun is plural, it does not need a preceding article.

> Alligators were loose at the zoo.

The **definite article** *(the)* is used to refer to specific nouns:

> The car pulled into our driveway.

Note that *the* should proceed all specific nouns regardless of whether they are singular or plural.

> The cars pulled into our driveway.

Comparative adjectives are used to compare nouns. When they are used in this way, they take on positive, comparative, or superlative form.

> The **positive** form is the normal form of the adjective:

>> Alicia is tall.

> The **comparative** form shows a comparison between two things:

>> Alicia is taller than Maria.

> **Superlative** form shows comparison between more than two things:

>> Alicia is the tallest girl in her class.

Usually, the comparative and superlative can be made by adding *–er* and *–est* to the positive form, but some verbs call for the helping verbs *more* or *most*. Other exceptions to the rule include adjectives like *bad*, which uses the comparative *worse* and the superlative *worst*.

An **adjective phrase** is not a bunch of adjectives strung together, but a group of words that describes a noun or pronoun and, thus, functions as an adjective. Very happy is an adjective phrase; so are way too hungry and passionate about traveling.

Adverbs

Adverbs have more functions than adjectives because they modify or qualify verbs, adjectives, or other adverbs as well as word groups that express a relation of place, time, circumstance, or cause. Therefore, adverbs answer any of the following questions: *How, when, where, why, in what way, how often, how much, in what condition,* and/or *to what degree. How good looking is he? He is <u>very</u> handsome.*

Here are some examples of adverbs for different situations:

- how: quickly
- when: daily
- where: there
- in what way: easily
- how often: often
- how much: much
- in what condition: badly
- what degree: hardly

As one can see, for some reason, many adverbs end in *-ly*.

Adverbs do things like emphasize (*really, simply,* and *so*), amplify (*heartily, completely,* and *positively*), and tone down (*almost, somewhat,* and *mildly*).

Adverbs also come in phrases.

> The dog ran as <u>though his life depended on it.</u>

Preposition

Prepositions are connecting words and, while there are only about 150 of them, they are used more often than any other individual groups of words. They describe relationships between other words. They are placed before a noun or pronoun, forming a phrase that modifies another word in the sentence. **Prepositional phrases** begin with a preposition and end with a noun or pronoun, the **object of the preposition.** *A pristine lake is <u>near the store</u> and <u>behind the bank</u>.*

Some commonly used prepositions are *about, after, anti, around, as, at, behind, beside, by, for, from, in, into, of, off, on, to,* and *with*.

Complex prepositions, which also come before a noun or pronoun, consist of two or three words such as *according to, in regards to,* and *because of.*

Prepositions show the relationship between different elements in a phrase or sentence and connect nouns or pronouns to other words in the sentence. Some examples of prepositions are words such as *after*, *at*, *behind*, *by*, *during*, *from*, *in*, *on*, *to*, and *with*.

> Let's go *to* class.

> Starry Night was painted *by* Vincent van Gogh *in* 1889.

Conjunctions

Conjunctions are vital words that connect words, phrases, thoughts, and ideas. Conjunctions show relationships between components. There are two types:

Coordinating conjunctions are the primary class of conjunctions placed between words, phrases, clauses, and sentences that are of equal grammatical rank; the coordinating conjunctions are *for*, *and*, *nor*, *but*, *or*, *yet*, and *so*. A useful memorization trick is to remember that the first letter of these conjunctions collectively spell the word *fanboys*.

> I need to go shopping, *but* I must be careful to leave enough money in the bank.
> She wore a black, red, *and* white shirt.

Subordinating conjunctions are the secondary class of conjunctions. They connect two unequal parts, one **main** (or **independent**) and the other *subordinate* (or *dependent*). I must go to the store *even though* I do not have enough money in the bank.

> *Because* I read the review, I do not want to go to the movie.

Notice that the presence of subordinating conjunctions makes clauses dependent. *I read the review* is an independent clause, but *because* makes the clause dependent. Thus, it needs an independent clause to complete the sentence.

Interjection

Interjections are words used to express emotion. Examples include *wow*, *ouch*, and *hooray*. Interjections are often separate from sentences; in those cases, the interjection is directly followed by an exclamation point. In other cases, the interjection is included in a sentence and followed by a comma. The punctuation plays a big role in the intensity of the emotion that the interjection is expressing. Using a comma or semicolon indicates less excitement than using an exclamation mark.

> *Wow*! Look at that sunset!

> Was it your birthday yesterday? *Oops*! I forgot.

Sentences

Types of Sentences

All sentences contain the same basic elements: a subject and a verb. The *subject* is who or what the sentence is about; the *verb* describes the subject's action or condition. However, these elements, subjects and verbs, can be combined in different ways. The following graphic describes the different types of sentence structures.

Sentence Structure	Independent Clauses	Dependent Clauses
Simple	1	0
Compound	2 or more	0
Complex	1	1 or more
Compound-Complex	2 or more	1 or more

A *simple sentence* expresses a complete thought and consists of one subject and verb combination:

> The children ate pizza.

The subject is *children*. The verb is *ate*.

Either the subject or the verb may be *compound*—that is, it could have more than one element:

> *The children and their parents* ate pizza.

> The children *ate pizza and watched a movie*.

All of these are still simple sentences. Despite having either compound subjects or compound verbs, each sentence still has only one subject and verb combination.

Compound sentences combine two or more simple sentences to form one sentence that has multiple subject-verb combinations:

> *The children ate pizza,* and *their parents watched a movie*.

This structure is comprised of two independent clauses: (1) *the children ate pizza* and (2) *their parents watched a movie.* Compound sentences join different subject-verb combinations using a comma and a coordinating conjunction.

> I called my mom, *but* she didn't answer the phone.

> The weather was stormy, *so* we canceled our trip to the beach.

A *complex sentence* consists of an independent clause and one or more dependent clauses. Dependent clauses join a sentence using *subordinating conjunctions*. Some examples of subordinating conjunctions are *although, unless, as soon as, since, while, when, because, if,* and *before.*

> I missed class yesterday *because* my mother was ill.

> *Before* traveling to a new country, you need to exchange your money to the local currency.

The order of clauses determines their punctuation. If the dependent clause comes first, it should be separated from the independent clause with a comma. However, if the complex sentence consists of an independent clause followed by a dependent clause, then a comma is not always necessary.

A *compound-complex sentence* can be created by joining two or more independent clauses with at least one dependent clause:

> After the earthquake struck, thousands of homes were destroyed, and many families were left without a place to live.

The first independent clause in the compound structure includes a dependent clause—*after the earthquake struck*. Thus, the structure is both complex and compound.

Other possible components of a sentence include descriptive words (adjectives or adverbs) that provide additional information called phrases or dependent clauses to the sentence but are not themselves complete sentences; independent clauses add more information to the sentence but could stand alone as their own sentence.

There isn't an overabundance of absolutes in grammar, but here is one: every sentence in the English language falls into one of four categories.

- Declarative: a simple statement that ends with a period

  The price of milk per gallon is the same as the price of gasoline.

- Imperative: a command, instruction, or request that ends with a period

  Buy milk when you stop to fill up your car with gas.

- Interrogative: a question that ends with a question mark

  Will you buy the milk?

- Exclamatory: a statement or command that expresses emotions like anger, urgency, or surprise and ends with an exclamation mark

  Buy the milk now!

Sentence Fragments

A *complete sentence* requires a verb and a subject that expresses a complete thought. Sometimes, the subject is omitted in the case of the implied *you*, used in sentences that are the command or imperative form—e.g., "Look!" or "Give me that." It is understood that the subject of the command is *you*, the listener or reader, so it is possible to have a structure without an explicit subject. Without these elements, though, the sentence is incomplete—it is a *sentence fragment*. While sentence fragments often occur in conversational English or creative writing, they are generally not appropriate in academic writing. Sentence fragments often occur when dependent clauses are not joined to an independent clause:

Sentence fragment: Because the airline overbooked the flight.

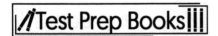

The sentence above is a dependent clause that does not express a complete thought. What happened as a result of this cause? With the addition of an independent clause, this now becomes a complete sentence:

> *Complete sentence*: Because the airline overbooked the flight, several passengers were unable to board.

Sentences fragments may also occur through improper use of conjunctions:

> I'm going to the Bahamas for spring break. And to New York City for New Year's Eve.

> While the first sentence above is a complete sentence, the second one is not because it is a prepositional phrase that lacks a subject [I] and a verb [am going]. Joining the two together with the coordinating conjunction forms one grammatically-correct sentence:

> I'm going to the Bahamas for spring break and to New York City for New Year's Eve.

Run-Ons

A *run-on* is a sentence with too many independent clauses that are improperly connected to each other:

> This winter has been very cold some farmers have suffered damage to their crops.

The sentence above has two subject-verb combinations. The first is "this winter has been"; the second is "some farmers have suffered." However, they are simply stuck next to each other without any punctuation or conjunction. Therefore, the sentence is a run-on.

Another type of run-on occurs when writers use inappropriate punctuation:

> This winter has been very cold, some farmers have suffered damage to their crops.

Though a comma has been added, this sentence is still not correct. When a comma alone is used to join two independent clauses, it is known as a **comma splice**. Without an appropriate conjunction, a comma cannot join two independent clauses by itself.

Run-on sentences can be corrected by either dividing the independent clauses into two or more separate sentences or inserting appropriate conjunctions and/or punctuation. The run-on sentence can be amended by separating each subject-verb pair into its own sentence:

> This winter has been very cold. Some farmers have suffered damage to their crops.

The run-on can also be fixed by adding a comma and conjunction to join the two independent clauses with each other:

> This winter has been very cold, so some farmers have suffered damage to their crops.

Parallelism

Parallel structure occurs when phrases or clauses within a sentence contain the same structure. Parallelism increases readability and comprehensibility because it is easy to tell which sentence elements are paired with each other in meaning.

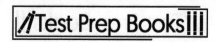

Jennifer enjoys cooking, knitting, and to spend time with her cat.

This sentence is not parallel because the items in the list appear in two different forms. Some are *gerunds,* which is the verb + ing: *cooking, knitting.* The other item uses the *infinitive* form, which is to + verb: *to spend.* To create parallelism, all items in the list may reflect the same form:

Jennifer enjoys cooking, knitting, and spending time with her cat.

All of the items in the list are now in gerund forms, so this sentence exhibits parallel structure. Here's another example:

The company is looking for employees who are responsible and with a lot of experience.

Again, the items that are listed in this sentence are not parallel. "Responsible" is an adjective, yet "with a lot of experience" is a prepositional phrase. The sentence elements do not utilize parallel parts of speech.

The company is looking for employees who are responsible and experienced.

"Responsible" and "experienced" are both adjectives, so this sentence now has parallel structure.

Dangling and Misplaced Modifiers

Modifiers enhance meaning by clarifying or giving greater detail about another part of a sentence. However, incorrectly-placed modifiers have the opposite effect and can cause confusion. A *misplaced modifier* is a modifier that is not located appropriately in relation to the word or phrase that it modifies:

Because he was one of the greatest thinkers of Renaissance Italy, John idolized Leonardo da Vinci.

In this sentence, the modifier is "because he was one of the greatest thinkers of Renaissance Italy," and the noun it is intended to modify is "Leonardo da Vinci." However, due to the placement of the modifier next to the subject, John, it seems as if the sentence is stating that John was a Renaissance genius, not Da Vinci.

John idolized Leonard da Vinci because he was one of the greatest thinkers of Renaissance Italy.

The modifier is now adjacent to the appropriate noun, clarifying which of the two men in this sentence is the greatest thinker.

Dangling modifiers modify a word or phrase that is not readily apparent in the sentence. That is, they "dangle" because they are not clearly attached to anything:

After getting accepted to college, Amir's parents were proud.

The modifier here, "after getting accepted to college," should modify who got accepted. The noun immediately following the modifier is "Amir's parents"—but they are probably not the ones who are going to college.

After getting accepted to college, Amir made his parents proud.

The subject of the sentence has been changed to Amir himself, and now the subject and its modifier are appropriately matched.

Inconsistent Verb Tense

Verb tense reflects when an action occurred or a state existed. For example, the tense known as *simple present* expresses something that is happening right now or that happens regularly:

> She *works* in a hospital.

Present continuous tense expresses something in progress. It is formed by to be + verb + -ing.

> Sorry, I can't go out right now. I *am doing* my homework.

Past tense is used to describe events that previously occurred. However, in conversational English, speakers often use present tense or a mix of past and present tense when relating past events because it gives the narrative a sense of immediacy. In formal written English, though, consistency in verb tense is necessary to avoid reader confusion.

> I traveled to Europe last summer. As soon as I stepped off the plane, I feel like I'm in a movie! I'm surrounded by quaint cafes and impressive architecture.

The passage above abruptly switches from past tense—*traveled*, *stepped*—to present tense—*feel*, *am surrounded*.

> I *traveled* to Europe last summer. As soon as I *stepped* off the plane, I *felt* like I was in a movie! I *was surrounded* by quaint cafes and impressive architecture.

All verbs are in past tense, so this passage now has consistent verb tense.

Clauses

Clauses are groups of words within a sentence that have both a subject and a verb. We can distinguish a clause from a phrase because phrases do not have both a subject and a verb. There are several types of clauses; clauses can be independent or dependent and can serve as a noun, an adjective, or an adverb.

An *independent clause* could stand alone as its own sentence if the rest of the sentence were not there. For example:

> *The party is on Tuesday* after the volleyball game is over.

> *I am excited to go to the party* because my best friend will be there.

A *dependent clause*, or subordinating clause, is the part of the sentence that gives supportive information but cannot create a proper sentence by itself. However, it will still have both a subject and a verb; otherwise, it is a phrase. In the example above, *after the volleyball game is over* and *because my best friend will be there* are dependent because they begin with the conjunctions *after* and *because*, and a proper sentence does not begin with a conjunction.

Noun clauses are groups of words that collectively form a noun. Look for the opening words *whether, which, what, that, who, how,* or *why*. For example:

> I had fun cooking *what we had for dinner last night.*

I'm going to track down *whoever ate my sandwich.*

Adjective clauses collectively form an adjective that modifies a noun or pronoun in the sentence. If you can remove the adjective clause and the leftovers create a standalone sentence, then the clause should be set off with commas, parentheses, or dashes. If you can remove the clause it is called nonrestrictive. If it can't be removed without ruining the sentence, then it is called restrictive and does not get set off with commas.

Jenna, *who hates to get wet,* fell into the pool. (Nonrestrictive)

The girl *who hates to get wet* fell into the pool. (Restrictive; the clause tells us which girl, and if removed there is confusion)

Adverbial clauses serve as an adverb in the sentence, modifying a verb, adjective, or other adverb. Look for the opening words *after, before, as, as if, although, because, if, since, so, so that, when, where, while,* or *unless.*

She lost her wallet after she left the theme park.

Her earring fell through the crack before she could catch it.

Phrases

A phrase is a group of words that go together but do not include both a subject and a verb. We use them to add information, explain something, or make the sentence easier for the reader to understand. Unlike clauses, phrases cannot ever stand alone as their own sentence if the rest of the sentence were not there. They do not form complete thoughts. There are noun phrases, prepositional phrases, verbal phrases, appositive phrases, and absolute phrases. Let's look at each of these.

Noun phrases: A noun phrase is a group of words built around a noun or pronoun that serves as a unit to form a noun in the sentence. Consider the following examples. The phrase is built around the underlined word. The entire phrase can be replaced by a noun or pronoun to test whether or not it is a noun phrase.

I like the chocolate chip ice cream. (I like it.)

I know all the shortest routes. (I know them.)

I met the best supporting actress. (I met her.)

Prepositional phrases: These are phrases that begin with a preposition and end with a noun or pronoun. We use them as a unit to form the adjective or adverb in the sentence. Prepositional phrases that introduce a sentence are called introductory prepositional phrases and are set off with commas.

I found the Frisbee *on the roof peak.* (Adverb; where it was found)

The girl *with the bright red hair* was prom queen. (Adjective; which girl)

Before the sequel, we wanted to watch the first movie. (Introductory phrase)

Verbal phrases: Some phrases look like verbs but do not serve as the verb in the sentence. These are called verbal phrases. There are three types: participial phrases, gerund phrases, and infinitive phrases.

Participial phrases start with a participle and modify nouns or pronouns; therefore, they act as the adjective in the sentence.

> *Beaten by the sun,* we searched for shade to sit in. (Modifies the pronoun *we*)

> The hikers, *being eaten by mosquitoes,* longed for repellant. (Modifies the noun *hikers*)

Gerund phrases often look like participles because they end in *-ing,* but they serve as the noun, not the adjective, in the sentence. Like any noun, we can use them as the subject or as the object of a verb or preposition in the sentence.

> *Eating green salad* is the best way to lose weight. (Subject)

> Sumo wrestlers are famous for *eating large quantities of food.* (Object)

Infinitive phrases often look like verbs because they start with the word *to,* but they serve as an adjective, adverb, or noun.

> *To survive the chill* is the goal of the Polar Bear Plunge. (Noun)

> A hot tub is at the scene *to warm up after the jump.* (Adverb)

> The jumpers have hot cocoa *to drink right away.* (Adjective)

Appositive phrases: We can use any of the above types of phrases to rename nouns or pronouns, and we call this an appositive phrase. Appositive phrases usually appear either just before or just after the noun or pronoun they are renaming. Appositive phrases are essential when the noun or pronoun is too general, and they are nonessential when they just add information.

> *The two famous brothers* Orville and Wilbur Wright invented the airplane. (Essential)

> Sarah Calysta, *my great grandmother,* is my namesake. (Nonessential)

Absolute phrases: When a participle comes after a noun and forms a phrase that is not otherwise part of the sentence, it's called an absolute phrase. Absolute phrases are not complete thoughts and cannot stand alone because they do not have a subject and a verb. They are not essential to the sentence in that they do not explain or add additional meaning to any other part of the sentence.

> *The engine roaring,* Jada closed her eyes and waited for the plane to take off.

> *The microphone crackling,* the flight attendant announced the delayed arrival.

Subject-Verb Agreement

In English, verbs must agree with the subject. The form of a verb may change depending on whether the subject is singular or plural, or whether it is first, second, or third person. For example, the verb *to be* has various forms:

> I <u>am </u>a student.

> You <u>are</u> a student.

> She <u>is</u> a student.

We <u>are</u> students.

They <u>are</u> students.

Errors occur when a verb does not agree with its subject. Sometimes, the error is readily apparent:

We is hungry.

Is is not the appropriate form of *to be* when used with the third person plural *we*.

We are hungry.

This sentence now has correct subject-verb agreement.

However, some cases are trickier, particularly when the subject consists of a lengthy noun phrase with many modifiers:

Students who are hoping to accompany the anthropology department on its annual summer trip to Ecuador needs to sign up by March 31st.

The verb in this sentence is *needs*. However, its subject is not the noun adjacent to it—Ecuador. The subject is the noun at the beginning of the sentence—students. Because *students* is plural, *needs* is the incorrect verb form.

Students who are hoping to accompany the anthropology department on its annual summer trip to Ecuador *need* to sign up by March 31st.

This sentence now uses correct agreement between *students* and *need*.

Another case to be aware of is a *collective noun*. A collective noun refers to a group of many things or people but can be singular in itself—e.g., family, committee, army, pair team, council, jury. Whether or not a collective noun uses a singular or plural verb depends on how the noun is being used. If the noun refers to the group performing a collective action as one unit, it should use a singular verb conjugation:

The family is moving to a new neighborhood.

The whole family is moving together in unison, so the singular verb form *is* is appropriate here.

The committee has made its decision.

The verb *has* and the possessive pronoun *its* both reflect the word *committee* as a singular noun in the sentence above; however, when a collective noun refers to the group as individuals, it can take a plural verb:

The newlywed pair spend every moment together.

This sentence emphasizes the love between two people in a pair, so it can use the plural verb *spend*.

The council are all newly elected members.

The sentence refers to the council in terms of its individual members and uses the plural verb *are*.

Overall though, American English is more likely to pair a collective noun with a singular verb, while British English is more likely to pair a collective noun with a plural verb.

Sentence Fluency

Learning and utilizing the mechanics of structure will encourage effective, professional results, and adding some creativity will elevate one's writing to a higher level.

First, let's review the basic elements of sentences.

A *sentence* is a set of words that make up a grammatical unit. The words must have certain elements and be spoken or written in a specific order to constitute a complete sentence that makes sense.

> 1. A sentence must have a *subject* (a noun or noun phrase). The subject tells whom or what the sentence is addressing (i.e. what it is about).

> 2. A sentence must have an *action* or *state of being* (*a verb*). To reiterate: A verb forms the main part of the predicate of a sentence. This means that it explains what the noun is doing.

> 3. A sentence must convey a complete thought.

Sometimes a sentence has two ideas that work together. For example, say the writer wants to make the following points:

> Seat belt laws have saved an estimated 50,000 lives.

> More lives are saved by seat belts every year.

These two ideas are directly related and appear to be of equal importance. Therefore they can be joined with a simple "and" as follows:

> Seat belt laws have saved an estimated 50,000 lives, and more lives are saved by seat belts every year.

The word *and* in the sentence helps the two ideas work together or, in other words, it "coordinates" them. It also serves as a junction where the two ideas come together, better known as a *conjunction*. Therefore, the word *and* is known as a *coordinating conjunction* (a word that helps bring two equal ideas together). Now that the ideas are joined together by a conjunction, they are known as *clauses*. Other coordinating conjunctions include *or*, *but*, and *so*.

Sometimes, however, two ideas in a sentence are *not* of equal importance:

> Seat belt laws have saved an estimated 50,000 lives.

> Many more lives could be saved with stronger federal seat belt laws.

In this case, combining the two with a coordinating conjunction (*and*) creates an awkward sentence:

> Seat belt laws have saved an estimated 50,000 lives, and many more lives could be saved with stronger federal seat belt laws.

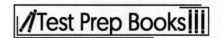

Now the writer uses a word to show the reader which clause is the most important (or the "boss") of the sentence:

> Although seat belt laws have saved an estimated 50,000 lives, many more lives could be saved with stronger federal seat belt laws.

In this example, the second clause is the key point that the writer wants to make, and the first clause works to set up that point. Since the first clause "works for" the second, it's called the *subordinate clause*. The word *although* tells the reader that this idea isn't as important as the clause that follows. This word is called the *subordinating conjunction*. Other subordinating conjunctions include *after*, *because*, *if*, *since*, *unless*, and many more. As mentioned before, it's easy to spot subordinate clauses because they don't stand on their own (as shown in this previous example):

> Although seat belt laws have saved an estimated 50,000 lives.

This is not a complete thought. It needs the other clause (called the *independent clause*) to make sense. On the test, when asked to choose the best subordinating conjunction for a sentence, look at the surrounding text. Choose the word that best allows the sentence to support the writer's argument.

Conjunctions are vital words that connect words, phrases, thoughts, and ideas. Conjunctions show relationships between components. There are two types: coordinating and subordinating.

Coordinating conjunctions are the primary class of conjunctions placed between words, phrases, clauses, and sentences that are of equal grammatical rank; the coordinating conjunctions are *for*, *and*, *nor*, *but*, *or*, *yet*, and *so*. A useful memorization trick is to remember that all the first letters of these conjunctions collectively spell the word fanboys.

> I need to go shopping, *but* I must be careful to leave enough money in the bank.
> She wore a black, red, *and* white shirt.

Subordinating conjunctions are the secondary class of conjunctions. They connect two unequal parts, one main (or independent) and the other subordinate (or dependent). I must go to the store *even though* I do not have enough money in the bank.

> *Because* I read the review, I do not want to go to the movie.

Notice that the presence of subordinating conjunctions makes clauses dependent. *I read the review* is an independent clause, but *because* makes the clause dependent. Thus, it needs an independent clause to complete the sentence.

Punctuation

End Punctuation

Periods (.) are used to end a sentence that is a statement (**declarative**) or a command (**imperative**). They should not be used in a sentence that asks a question or is an exclamation. Periods are also used in abbreviations, which are shortened versions of words.

- Declarative: The boys refused to go to sleep.
- Imperative: Walk down to the bus stop.
- Abbreviations: Joan Roberts, M.D., Apple Inc., Mrs. Adamson
- If a sentence ends with an abbreviation, it is inappropriate to use two periods. It should end with a single period after the abbreviation.

    The chef gathered the ingredients for the pie, which included apples, flour, sugar, etc.

Question marks *(?)* are used with direct questions (**interrogative**). An **indirect question** can use a period:

    Interrogative: When does the next bus arrive?

    Indirect Question: I wonder when the next bus arrives.

An **exclamation point** *(!)* is used to show strong emotion or can be used as an interjection. This punctuation should be used sparingly in formal writing situations.

    What an amazing shot!

    Whoa!

Commas

A **comma** (,) is the punctuation mark that signifies a pause—breath—between parts of a sentence. It denotes a break of flow. Proper comma usage helps readers understand the writer's intended emphasis of ideas.

In a complex sentence—one that contains a **subordinate** (dependent) clause or clauses—the use of a comma is dictated by where the subordinate clause is located. If the subordinate clause is located before the main clause, a comma is needed between the two clauses.

    I will not pay for the steak, *because I don't have that much money.*

Generally, if the subordinate clause is placed after the main clause, no punctuation is needed.

    I did well on my exam because I studied two hours the night before.

Notice how the last clause is dependent because it requires the earlier independent clauses to make sense.

Use a comma on both sides of an interrupting phrase.

I will pay for the ice cream, *chocolate and vanilla*, and then will eat it all myself.

The words forming the phrase in italics are nonessential (extra) information. To determine if a phrase is nonessential, try reading the sentence without the phrase and see if it's still coherent.

A comma is not necessary in this next sentence because no interruption—nonessential or extra information—has occurred. Read sentences aloud when uncertain.

I will pay for his chocolate and vanilla ice cream and then will eat it all myself.

If the nonessential phrase comes at the beginning of a sentence, a comma should only go at the end of the phrase. If the phrase comes at the end of a sentence, a comma should only go at the beginning of the phrase.

Other types of interruptions include the following:

- interjections: Oh no, I am not going.
- abbreviations: Barry Potter, M.D., specializes in heart disorders.
- direct addresses: Yes, Claudia, I am tired and going to bed.
- parenthetical phrases: His wife, lovely as she was, was not helpful.
- transitional phrases: Also, it is not possible.

The second comma in the following sentence is called an **Oxford comma**.

I will pay for ice cream, syrup, and pop.

It is a comma used after the second-to-last item in a series of three or more items. It comes before the word *or* or *and*. Not everyone uses the Oxford comma; it is optional, but many believe it is needed. The comma functions as a tool to reduce confusion in writing. So, if omitting the Oxford comma would cause confusion, then it's best to include it.

Commas are used in math to mark the place of thousands in numerals, breaking them up so they are easier to read. Other uses for commas are in dates (*March 19, 2016*), letter greetings (*Dear Sally,*), and in between cities and states (*Louisville, KY*).

Semicolons

A **semicolon** *(;)* is used to connect ideas in a sentence in some way. There are three main ways to use semicolons.

Link two independent clauses without the use of a coordinating conjunction:

I was late for work again; I'm definitely going to get fired.

Link two independent clauses with a transitional word:

The songs were all easy to play; therefore, he didn't need to spend too much time practicing.

Between items in a series that are already separated by commas or if necessary to separate lengthy items in a list:

> Starbucks has locations in Media, PA; Swarthmore, PA; and Morton, PA.

> Several classroom management issues presented in the study: the advent of a poor teacher persona in the context of voice, dress, and style; teacher follow-through from the beginning of the school year to the end; and the depth of administrative support, including ISS and OSS protocol.

Colons

A **colon** (:) is used after an independent clause to present an explanation or draw attention to what comes next in the sentence. There are several uses.

Explanations of ideas:

> They soon learned the hardest part about having a new baby: sleep deprivation.

Lists of items:

> Shari picked up all the supplies she would need for the party: cups, plates, napkins, balloons, streamers, and party favors.

Time, subtitles, general salutations:

> The time is 7:15.

> I read a book entitled *Pluto: A Planet No More*.

> To whom it may concern:

Parentheses and Dashes

Parentheses are half-round brackets that look like this: ( ). They set off a word, phrase, or sentence that is an afterthought, explanation, or side note relevant to the surrounding text but not essential. A pair of commas is often used to set off this sort of information, but parentheses are generally used for information that would not fit well within a sentence or that the writer deems not important enough to be structurally part of the sentence.

> The picture of the heart (see above) shows the major parts you should memorize.
> Mount Everest is one of three mountains in the world that are over 28,000 feet high (K2 and Kanchenjunga are the other two).

See how the sentences above are complete without the parenthetical statements? In the first example, *see above* would not have fit well within the flow of the sentence. The second parenthetical statement could have been a separate sentence, but the writer deemed the information not pertinent to the topic.

The **em-dash** (—) is a mark longer than a hyphen used as a punctuation mark in sentences and to set apart a relevant thought. Even after plucking out the line separated by the dash marks, the sentence will be intact and make sense.

> Looking out the airplane window at the landmarks—Lake Clarke, Thompson Community College, and the bridge—she couldn't help but feel excited to be home.

The dashes use is similar to that of parentheses or a pair of commas. So, what's the difference? Many believe that using dashes makes the clause within them stand out while using parentheses is subtler. It's advised to not use dashes when commas could be used instead.

Ellipses

An **ellipsis** (…) consists of three handy little dots that can speak volumes on behalf of irrelevant material. Writers use them in place of words, lines, phrases, list content, or paragraphs that might just as easily have been omitted from a passage of writing. This can be done to save space or to focus only on the specifically relevant material.

> Exercise is good for some unexpected reasons. Watkins writes, "Exercise has many benefits such as…reducing cancer risk."

In the example above, the ellipsis takes the place of the other benefits of exercise that are more expected.

The ellipsis may also be used to show a pause in sentence flow.

> "I'm wondering...how this could happen," Dylan said in a soft voice.

Quotation Marks

Double quotation marks are used at the beginning and end of a direct quote. They are also used with certain titles and to indicate that a term being used is slang or referenced in the sentence. Quotation marks should not be used with an indirect quote. Single quotation marks are used to indicate a quote within a quote.

> Direct quote: "The weather is supposed to be beautiful this week," she said.

> Indirect quote: One of the customers asked if the sale prices were still in effect.

> Quote within a quote: "My little boy just said 'Mama, I want cookie,'" Maria shared.

Titles: Quotation marks should also be used to indicate titles of short works or sections of larger works, such as chapter titles. Other works that use quotation marks include poems, short stories, newspaper articles, magazine articles, web page titles, and songs.

> "The Road Not Taken" is my favorite poem by Robert Frost.

> "What a Wonderful World" is one of my favorite songs.

Specific or emphasized terms: Quotation marks can also be used to indicate a technical term or to set off a word that is being discussed in a sentence. Quotation marks can also indicate sarcasm.

> The new step, called "levigation," is a very difficult technique.

> He said he was "hungry" multiple times, but he only ate two bites.

Use with other punctuation: The use of quotation marks with other punctuation varies, depending on the role of the ending or separating punctuation.

In American English, periods and commas always go inside the quotation marks:

> "This is the last time you are allowed to leave early," his boss stated.

> The newscaster said, "We have some breaking news to report."

Question marks or exclamation points go inside the quotation marks when they are part of a direct quote:

> The doctor shouted, "Get the crash cart!"

When the question mark or exclamation point is part of the sentence, not the quote, it should be placed outside of the quotation marks:

> Was it Jackie that said, "Get some potatoes at the store"?

Apostrophes

This punctuation mark, the **apostrophe** (') is a versatile mark. It has several different functions:

- Quotes: Apostrophes are used when a second quote is needed within a quote.

  - In my letter to my friend, I wrote, "The girl had to get a new purse, and guess what Mary did? She said, 'I'd like to go with you to the store.' I knew Mary would buy it for her."

- Contractions: Another use for an apostrophe in the quote above is a contraction. *I'd is used for I would.*

- Possession: An apostrophe followed by the letter s shows possession (Mary's purse). If the possessive word is plural, the apostrophe generally just follows the word. Not all possessive pronouns require apostrophes.

  - The trees' leaves are all over the ground.

Hyphens

The **hyphen** (-) is a small hash mark that can be used to join words to show that they are linked.

Hyphenate two words that work together as a single adjective (a compound adjective).

> honey-covered biscuits

Some words always require hyphens, even if not serving as an adjective.

merry-go-round

Hyphens always go after certain prefixes like *anti-* & *all-*.

Hyphens should also be used when the absence of the hyphen would cause a strange vowel combination (*semi-engineer*) or confusion. For example, *re-collect* should be used to describe something being gathered twice rather than being written as *recollect*, which means to remember.

Spelling and Capitalization

Spelling

Both spoken and written words have rhythm that might be defined as *inflection*. This serves to help writers in their choice of words, expression, and correct spelling. When creating original works, do at least one reading aloud. Some inflection is intrinsic to the words, some are added by writers, and some will be inferred when later read. If the written words are not spelled correctly, then what the author intended is not conveyed. Use rhythm as a spelling tool.

Saying and listening to a word serves as the beginning of knowing how to spell it. Keep these subsequent guidelines in mind, remembering there are often exceptions, because the English language is replete with them.

Guideline #1: Syllables must have a vowel

Every syllable in every English word has a vowel. Examples: d*o*g, h*a*yst*a*ck, *a*nsw*e*r*i*ng, *a*bst*e*nt*iou*s (the longest word that uses the five vowels in order), and s*i*mple.

In addition to this vowel guideline is a built-in bonus: Guideline #1 helps one see whether the word looks right.

Guideline #2: The silent final -e

The final word example in Guideline #1, s*i*mple, provides the opportunity to see another guideline with multiple types:

- Because every syllable has a vowel, words like *simple* require the final silent -*e*.

- In a word that has a vowel-consonant-e combination like the short, simple word at*e*, the silent –*e* at the end shapes the sound of the earlier vowel. The technical term for this is it "makes the vowel say its name." There are thousands of examples of this guideline; just for starters, look at cut*e*, mat*e*, and tot*e*.

- Let's *dance*...after we leave the *range!* Look what the final silent –*e* does for the –*c* and –*g*: each provides the word's soft sound.

- Other than to *rev* a car's engine, are there other words that ends in a –*v?* How about a word that ends in a –*u?* Well some like their cheese ble*u*, there's one, but, while there are more (well, okay, *you*), they are few and far between, and consider words having the ending of the letter –*i*. Yes, English words generally do not end in –*v's*, –*u's*, and –*i's*, so silent –*e* to the rescue! Note that it does not change the pronunciation. Examples: believ*e*, lov*e*, and activ*e*; blu*e*, and tru*e*; and two very important –*i* examples, browni*e* and cooki*e*. (Exceptions to this rule are generally words from other languages.)

Guideline #3: The long and short of it

When the vowel has a short vowel sound as in *mad* or *bed*, only the single vowel is needed. If the word has a long vowel sound, add another vowel, either alongside it or separated by a consonant: bed/be*a*d; mad/ma*d*e. When the second vowel is separated by two spaces—*madder*—it does not affect the first vowel's sound.

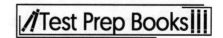

Guideline #4: What about the –fixes (pre- and suf-)?

A *prefix* is a word, letter, or number that is placed before another. It adjusts or qualifies the root word's meaning. When written alone, prefixes are followed by a dash to indicate that the root word follows. Some of the most common prefixes are the following:

Prefix	Meaning	Example
dis-	not or opposite of	disabled
in-, im-, il-, ir-	not	illiterate
re-	again	return
un-	not	unpredictable
anti-	against	antibacterial
fore-	before	forefront
mis-	wrongly	misunderstand
non-	not	nonsense
over-	more than normal	overabundance
pre-	before	preheat
super-	above	superman

A suffix is a letter or group of letters added at the end of a word to form another word. The word created from the root and suffix is either a different tense of the same root (*help + ed = helped*) or a new word (*help + ful = helpful*). When written alone, suffixes are preceded by a dash to indicate that the root word comes before.

Some of the most common suffixes are the following:

Suffix	Meaning	Example
ed	makes a verb past tense	wash*ed*
ing	makes a verb a present participle verb	wash*ing*
ly	to make characteristic of	love*ly*
s/es	to make more than one	chairs, box*es*
able	can be done	deplor*able*
al	having characteristics of	comic*al*
est	comparative	great*est*
ful	full of	wonder*ful*
ism	belief in	commun*ism*
less	without	faithless
ment	action or process	accomplish*ment*
ness	state of	happi*ness*
ize, ise	to render, to make	steril*ize*, advert*ise*
cede/ceed/sede	go	concede, proceed, supersede

Here are some helpful tips:

- When adding a suffix that starts with a vowel (for example, -ed) to a one-syllable root whose vowel has a short sound and ends in a consonant (for example, *stun*), double the final consonant of the root (*n*).

    stun + ed = stun*n*ed

    Exception: If the past tense verb ends in *x* such as *box*, do not double the *x*.

    box + ed = boxed

- If adding a suffix that starts with a vowel (-*er*) to a multi-syllable word ending in a consonant (*begin*), double the consonant (*n*).

    begin + er = begin*n*er

- If a short vowel is followed by two or more consonants in a word such as *i+t+c+h = itch,* do <u>not</u> double the last consonant.

    itch + ed = itched

- If adding a suffix that starts with a vowel (-*ing*) to a word ending in *e* (for example, *name*), that word's final *e* is generally (but not always) dropped.

    name + ing = naming
    exception: manage + able = manag*e*able

- If adding a suffix that starts with a consonant (-*ness*) to a word ending in *e* (*complete*), the *e* generally (but not always) remains.

    complete + ness = completeness
    exception: judge + ment = judgment

There is great diversity on handling words that end in *y.* For words ending in a vowel + y, nothing changes in the original word.

    play + ed = played

For words ending in a consonant + y, change the y to i when adding any suffix except for –*ing*.

    marry + ed = married
    marry + ing = marrying

Guideline #5: Which came first, the –i or the –e?

"When the letter 'c' you spy, put the 'e' before the 'i.' (Do not be) dec*ei*ved; when the letter 's' you see, put the 'i' before the 'e' (or you might be under) s*ie*ge." This old adage still holds up today regarding words where the "c" and "s" *precede* the "i." Another variation is, "'*i*' before '*e*' except after '*c*' or when sounded as '*a*' as in *neighbor* or *weigh*." Keep in mind that these are only guidelines and that there are always exceptions to every rule.

Guideline #6: Vowels in the right order

A different helpful ditty is, "When two vowels go walking, the first one does the talking." Usually, when two vowels are in a row, the first one often has a long vowel sound and the other is silent. An example is *team*.

When having difficulty spelling words, determine a strategy to help. Work on pronunciations, play word games like Scrabble or Words with Friends, and consider using phonics (sounding words out by slowly and surely stating each syllable). Try using repetition and memorization and picturing the words. Try memory aids like making up silly things. See what works best. For disorders such as dyslexia, know that there are accommodations to help.

Use computer spellcheck; however, do not *rely on* computer spellcheck.

Common Usage Mistakes

Its and It's

These pronouns are some of the most confused in the English language as most possessives contain the suffix –'s. However, for *it*, it is the opposite. *Its* is a possessive pronoun:

> The government is reassessing *its* spending plan.

It's is a contraction of the words *it is*:

> *It's* snowing outside.

Saw and Seen

Saw and *seen* are both conjugations of the verb *to see*, but they express different verb tenses. *Saw* is used in the simple past tense. *Seen* is the past participle form of *to see* and can be used in all perfect tenses.

> I seen her yesterday.

This sentence is incorrect. Because it expresses a completed event from a specified point in time in the past, it should use simple past tense:

> I *saw* her yesterday.

This sentence uses the correct verb tense. Here's how the past participle is used correctly:

> I *have seen* her before.

The meaning in this sentence is slightly changed to indicate an event from an unspecific time in the past. In this case, present perfect is the appropriate verb tense to indicate an unspecified past experience. Present perfect conjugation is created by combining *to have* + past participle.

Then and Than

Then is generally used as an adverb indicating something that happened next in a sequence or as the result of a conditional situation:

> We parked the car and *then* walked to the restaurant.

> If enough people register for the event, *then* we can begin planning.

Than is a conjunction indicating comparison:

> This watch is more expensive *than* that one.

> The bus departed later *than* I expected.

They're, Their, and There

They're is a contraction of the words *they are*:

> *They're* moving to Ohio next week.

Their is a possessive pronoun:

> The baseball players are training for *their* upcoming season.

There can function as multiple parts of speech, but it is most commonly used as an adverb indicating a location:

> Let's go to the concert! Some great bands are playing *there*.

Insure and Ensure

These terms are both verbs. *Insure* means to guarantee something against loss, harm, or damage, usually through an insurance policy that offers monetary compensation:

> The robbers made off with her prized diamond necklace, but luckily it was *insured* for one million dollars.

Ensure means to make sure, to confirm, or to be certain:

> *Ensure* that you have your passport before entering the security checkpoint.

Accept and Except

Accept is a verb meaning to take or agree to something:

> I would like to *accept* your offer of employment.

Except is a preposition that indicates exclusion:

> I've been to every state in America *except* Hawaii.

Affect and Effect

Affect is a verb meaning to influence or to have an impact on something:

> The amount of rainfall during the growing season *affects* the flavor of wine produced from these grapes.

Effect can be used as either a noun or a verb. As a noun, *effect* is synonymous with a result:

> If we implement the changes, what will the *effect* be on our profits?

As a verb, *effect* means to bring about or to make happen:

> In just a few short months, the healthy committee has *effected* real change in school nutrition.

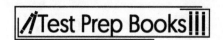

Capitalization

Here's a non-exhaustive list of things that should be capitalized.

- The first word of every sentence
- The first word of every line of poetry
- The first letter of proper nouns (World War II)
- Holidays (Valentine's Day)
- The days of the week and months of the year (Tuesday, March)
- The first word, last word, and all major words in the titles of books, movies, songs, and other creative works (In the novel, *To Kill a Mockingbird*, note that *a* is lowercase since it's not a major word, but *to* is capitalized since it's the first word of the title.)
- Titles when preceding a proper noun (President Roberto Gonzales, Aunt Judy)

When simply using a word such as president or secretary, though, the word is not capitalized.

Officers of the new business must include a president and treasurer.

Seasons—spring, fall, etc.—are not capitalized.

North, south, east, and west are capitalized when referring to regions but are not when being used for directions. In general, if it's preceded by the it should be capitalized.

I'm from the South.

I drove south.

Here are some additional rules about capitalization:

- Capitalize the first word in a sentence and the first word in a quotation:

    The realtor showed them the house.

    Robert asked, "When can we get together for dinner again?"

- Capitalize proper nouns and words derived from them:

    We are visiting Germany in a few weeks.

    We will stay with our German relatives on our trip.

- Capitalize days of the week, months of the year, and holidays:

    The book club meets the last Thursday of every month.

    The baby is due in June.

    I decided to throw a Halloween party this year.

- Capitalize the main words in titles (referred to as *title case*), but not the articles, conjunctions, or prepositions:

    A Raisin in the Sun

    To Kill a Mockingbird

- Capitalize directional words that are used as names, but not when referencing a direction:

    The North won the Civil War.

    After making a left, go north on Rt. 476.

    She grew up on the West Coast.

    The winds came in from the west.

- Capitalize titles that go with names:

    Mrs. McFadden   Sir Alec Guinness   Lt. Madeline Suarez

- Capitalize familial relationships when referring to a *specific* person:

    I worked for my Uncle Steven last summer.

    Did you work for your uncle last summer?

Organization

Good writing is not merely a random collection of sentences. No matter how well written, sentences must relate and coordinate appropriately with one another. If not, the writing seems random, haphazard, and disorganized. Therefore, good writing must be organized, where each sentence fits a larger context and relates to the sentences around it.

Transition Words

The writer should act as a guide, showing the reader how all the sentences fit together. Consider this example concerning seat belts:

> Seat belts save more lives than any other automobile safety feature. Many studies show that airbags save lives as well. Not all cars have airbags. Many older cars don't. Air bags aren't entirely reliable. Studies show that in 15 percent of accidents, airbags don't deploy as designed. Seat belt malfunctions are extremely rare.

There's nothing wrong with any of these sentences individually, but together they're disjointed and difficult to follow. The best way for the writer to communicate information is through the use of transition words. Here are examples of transition words and phrases that tie sentences together, enabling a more natural flow:

- To show causality: as a result, therefore, and consequently
- To compare and contrast: *however*, *but*, and *on the other hand*
- To introduce examples: *for example*, *namely*, and *including*
- To show order of importance: *foremost*, *primarily*, *secondly*, and *lastly*

Note that this is not a complete list of transitions. There are many more that can be used; however, most fit into these or similar categories. The important point is that the words should clearly show the relationship between sentences, supporting information, and the main idea.

Here is an update to the previous example using transition words. These changes make it easier to read and bring clarity to the writer's points:

> Seat belts save more lives than any other automobile safety feature. Many studies show that airbags save lives as well; however, not all cars have airbags. For example, some older cars don't. Furthermore, air bags aren't entirely reliable. For example, studies show that in 15 percent of accidents, airbags don't deploy as designed, but, on the other hand, seat belt malfunctions are extremely rare.

Also, be prepared to analyze whether the writer is using the best transition word or phrase for the situation. Take this sentence for example: "As a result, seat belt malfunctions are extremely rare." This sentence doesn't make sense in the context above because the writer is trying to show the contrast between seat belts and airbags, not the causality.

Relevance of Content

A reader must be able to evaluate the argument or point the author is trying to make and determine if it is adequately supported. The first step is to determine the main idea. The main idea is what the author wants to say about a specific topic. The next step is to locate the supporting details. An author uses supporting details to illustrate the main idea. These are the details that provide evidence or examples to help make a point. Supporting details often appear in the form of quotations, paraphrasing, or analysis. Test takers should then examine the text to make sure the author connects details and analysis to the main point. These steps are crucial to understanding the text and evaluating how well the author presents his or her argument and evidence. The following graphic demonstrates the connection between the main idea and the supporting details.

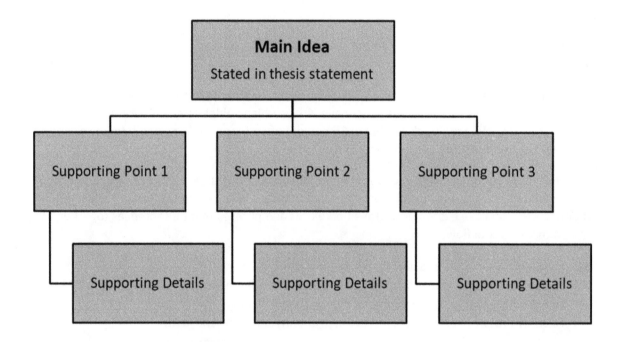

It is important to evaluate the author's supporting details to be sure that they are credible, provide evidence of the author's point, and directly support the main idea. Critical readers examine the facts used to support an author's argument and check those facts against other sources to be sure the facts are correct. They also check the validity of the sources used to be sure those sources are credible, academic, and/or peer- reviewed. A strong argument uses valid, measurable facts to support ideas.

Developing a Well-Organized Paragraph

Forming Paragraphs

A good *paragraph* should have the following characteristics:

- Be logical with organized sentences
- Have a *unified* purpose within itself
- Use sentences as *building blocks*
- Be a *distinct section* of a piece of writing
- Present a *single theme* introduced by a *topic sentence*
- Maintain a *consistent flow* through subsequent, relevant, well-placed sentences
- *Tell a story* of its own or have its own purpose, yet connect with what is written before and after
- Enlighten, entertain, and/or inform

Though certainly not set in stone, the length should be a consideration for the reader's sake, not merely for the sake of the topic. When paragraphs are especially short, the reader might experience an irregular, uneven effect; when they're much longer than 250 words, the reader's attention span, and probably their retention, is challenged. While a paragraph can technically be a sentence long, a good rule of thumb is for paragraphs to be at least three sentences long and no more than ten sentence long. An optimal word length is 100 to 250 words.

Coherent Paragraphs

Coherence is simply defined as the quality of being logical and consistent. In order to have coherent paragraphs, therefore, authors must be logical and consistent in their writing, whatever the document might be. Two words are helpful to understanding coherence: flow and relationship. Transitions are often referred to as being the "glue" to put organized thoughts together. Now, let's look at the topic sentence from which flow and relationship originate.

The topic sentence, usually the first in a paragraph, holds the essential features that will be brought forth in the paragraph. It is also here that authors either grab or lose readers. It may be the only writing that a reader encounters from that writer, so it is a good idea to summarize and represent ideas accurately.

The coherent paragraph has a logical order. It utilizes transitional words and phrases, parallel sentence structure, clear pronoun references, and reasonable repetition of key words and phrases. It is important to use common sense for repetition, consider synonyms for variety, and be consistent in verb tense whenever possible.

When writers have accomplished their paragraph's purpose, they prepare it to receive the next paragraph. While writing, read the paragraph over, edit, examine, evaluate, and make changes accordingly. Possibly, a paragraph has gone on too long. If that occurs, it needs to be broken up into other paragraphs, or the length should be reduced. If a paragraph didn't fully accomplish its purpose, consider revising it.

Main Point of a Paragraph

The main point of a paragraph is *the* point all the lesser important points should lead up to, and it should be summed up in the topic sentence.

Sometimes there is a fine line between a paragraph's topic sentence and its main point. In fact, they actually might be one and the same. Often, though, they are two separate but closely related aspects of the same paragraph.

Depending upon writer's purpose, the topic sentence or the paragraph's main point might not be fully revealed until the paragraph's conclusion.

Sometimes, while developing paragraphs, authors deviate from the main point, which means they have to delete and rework their materials to stay on point.

Examining Paragraphs

Throughout this text, composing and combining sentences, using basic grammar skills, employing rules and guidelines, identifying differing points of view, using appropriate context, constructing accurate word usage, and discerning correct punctuation have all been discussed. Whew! The types of sentences, patterns, transitions, and overall structure have been covered as well.

While authors write, thoughts coalesce to form words on "paper" (aka a computer screen). Authors strategically place those thoughts in sentences to give them "voice" in an orderly manner, and then they manipulate them into cohesive sentences for cohesion to express ideas. Like a hunk of modeling clay, sentences can be worked and reworked until they cooperate and say what was originally intended.

Before calling a paragraph complete, identify its main point, making sure that related sentences stay on point. Pose questions such as, "Did I sufficiently develop the main point? Did I say it succinctly enough? Did I give it time to develop?"

Let's examine the following two paragraphs, each an example of a movie review. Read them and form a critique.

Example 1: *Eddie the Eagle* is a movie about a struggling athlete. Eddie was crippled at birth. He had a lot of therapy and he had a dream. Eddie trained himself for the Olympics. He went far away to learn how to ski jump. It was hard for him, but he persevered. He got a coach and kept trying. He qualified for the Olympics. He was the only one from Britain who could jump. When he succeeded, they named him, "Eddie the Eagle."

Example 2: The last movie I saw in the theater was *Eddie the Eagle,* a story of extraordinary perseverance inspired by real life events. Eddie was born in England with a birth defect that he slowly but surely overcame, but not without trial and error (not the least of which was his father's perpetual *dis*couragement). In fact, the old man did everything to get him to give up, but Eddie was dogged beyond anyone in the neighborhood; in fact, maybe beyond anyone in the whole town or even the whole world! Eddie, simply, did not know to quit. As he grew up, so did his dream; a strange one, indeed, for someone so unaccomplished: to compete in the Winter Olympics as a ski jumper (which he knew absolutely nothing about). Eddie didn't just keep on dreaming about it. He actually went to Germany and *worked* at it, facing unbelievable odds, defeats, and put-downs by Dad and the other Men in Charge, aka the Olympic decision-makers. Did that stop him? No way! Eddie got a coach and persevered. Then, when he failed, he persevered some more, again and again. You should be able to open up a dictionary, look at the word "persevere," and see a picture of Eddie the Eagle because, when everybody told him he couldn't, he did. The result? He is forever dubbed, "Eddie the Eagle."

Both reviews tell something about the movie *Eddie the Eagle*. Does one motivate the reader to want to see the movie more than the other? Does one just provide a few facts while the other paints a virtual picture of the movie? Does one give a carrot and the other a rib eye steak, mashed potatoes, and chocolate silk pie?

Paragraphs sometimes only give facts. Sometimes that's appropriate and all that is needed. Sometimes, though, writers want to paint a picture. Writers must "see" the painting come to life. To do so, pick a familiar topic, write a simple sentence, and add to it. Pretend, for example, there's a lovely view. What does one see? Is it a lake? Try again – picture it as though it were the sea! Visualize a big ship sailing out there. Is it sailing away or approaching? Who is on it? Is it dangerous? Is it night and are there pirates on board? Uh-oh! Did one just jump ship and start swimming toward shore?

Recognizing Logical Transitions

Even if the writer includes plenty of information to support their point, the writing is only coherent when the information is in a logical order. First, the writer should introduce the main idea, whether for a paragraph, a section, or the entire piece. Second, they should present evidence to support the main idea

by using transitional language. This shows the reader how the information relates to the main idea and to the sentences around it. The writer should then take time to interpret the information, making sure necessary connections are obvious to the reader. Finally, the writer can summarize the information in a closing section.

The logical order of a piece is supported by certain transitions that signal information is related or linked in a logical way. These transitions can include words like however, consequently, and likewise.

Though most writing follows this pattern, it isn't a set rule. Sometimes writers change the order for effect. For example, the writer can begin with a surprising piece of supporting information to grab the reader's attention, and then transition to the main idea. Thus, if a passage doesn't follow the logical order, don't immediately assume it's wrong. However, most writing usually settles into a logical sequence after a nontraditional beginning.

Diction and Idioms

Idiomatic Usage

A figure of speech (sometimes called an idiom) is a rhetorical device. It's a phrase that is not intended to be taken literally.

When the writer uses a figure of speech, their intention must be clear if it's to be used effectively. Some phrases can be interpreted in a number of ways, causing confusion for the reader. Look for clues to the writer's true intention to determine the best replacement. Likewise, some figures of speech may seem out of place in a more formal piece of writing. To show this, here is another example involving seat belts:

> Seat belts save more lives than any other automobile safety feature. Many studies show that airbags save lives as well, however not all cars have airbags. For example, some older cars don't. In addition, air bags aren't entirely reliable. For example, studies show that in 15 percent of accidents, airbags don't deploy as designed, but, on the other hand, seat belt malfunctions happen once in a blue moon.

Most people know that "once in a blue moon" refers to something that rarely happens. However, because the rest of the paragraph is straightforward and direct, using this figurative phrase distracts the reader. In this example, the earlier version is much more effective.

Now it's important to take a moment and review the meaning of the word *literally*. This is because it's one of the most misunderstood and misused words in the English language. *Literally* means that something is exactly what it says it is, and there can be no interpretation or exaggeration. Unfortunately, *literally* is often used for emphasis as in the following example:

> This morning, I literally couldn't get out of bed.

This sentence meant to say that the person was extremely tired and wasn't able to get up. However, the sentence can't *literally* be true unless that person was tied down to the bed, paralyzed, or affected by a strange situation that the writer (most likely) didn't intend. Here's another example:

> I literally died laughing.

The writer tried to say that something was very funny. However, unless they're writing this from beyond the grave, it can't *literally* be true.

Note that this doesn't mean that writers can't use figures of speech. The colorful use of language and idioms make writing more interesting and draw in the reader. However, for these kinds of expressions to be used correctly, they cannot include the word *literally*.

Style, Tone, and Mood

Style, tone, and mood are often thought to be the same thing. Though they're closely related, there are important differences to keep in mind. The easiest way to do this is to remember that style "creates and affects" tone and mood. More specifically, style is how the writer uses words to create the desired tone and mood for their writing.

44

Style

Style can include any number of technical writing choices. A few examples of style choices include:

- Sentence Construction: When presenting facts, does the writer use shorter sentences to create a quicker sense of the supporting evidence, or do they use longer sentences to elaborate and explain the information?

- Technical Language: Does the writer use jargon to demonstrate their expertise in the subject, or do they use ordinary language to help the reader understand things in simple terms?

- Formal Language: Does the writer refrain from using contractions such as *won't* or *can't* to create a more formal tone, or do they use a colloquial, conversational style to connect to the reader?

- Formatting: Does the writer use a series of shorter paragraphs to help the reader follow a line of argument, or do they use longer paragraphs to examine an issue in great detail and demonstrate their knowledge of the topic?

On the test, examine the writer's style and how their writing choices affect the way the text comes across.

Tone

Tone refers to the writer's attitude toward the subject matter. Tone is usually explained in terms of a work of fiction. For example, the tone conveys how the writer feels about their characters and the situations in which they're involved. Nonfiction writing is sometimes thought to have no tone at all; however, this is incorrect.

A lot of nonfiction writing has a neutral tone, which is an important tone for the writer to take. A neutral tone demonstrates that the writer is presenting a topic impartially and letting the information speak for itself. On the other hand, nonfiction writing can be just as effective and appropriate if the tone isn't neutral. For example, let's look at the seat belt example again:

> Seat belts save more lives than any other automobile safety feature. Many studies show that airbags save lives as well; however, not all cars have airbags. For example, some older cars don't. Furthermore, air bags aren't entirely reliable. For example, studies show that in 15 percent of accidents airbags don't deploy as designed, but, on the other hand, seat belt malfunctions are extremely rare. The number of highway fatalities has plummeted since laws requiring seat belt usage were enacted.

In this passage, the writer mostly chooses to retain a neutral tone when presenting information. If the writer would instead include their own personal experience of losing a friend or family member in a car accident, the tone would change dramatically. The tone would no longer be neutral and would show that the writer has a personal stake in the content, allowing them to interpret the information in a different way. When analyzing tone, consider what the writer is trying to achieve in the text and how they *create* the tone using style.

Mood

Mood refers to the feelings and atmosphere that the writer's words create for the reader. Like tone, many nonfiction texts can have a neutral mood. To return to the previous example, if the writer would choose to include information about a person they know being killed in a car accident, the text would suddenly carry an emotional component that is absent in the previous example. Depending on how they present the information, the writer can create a sad, angry, or even hopeful mood. When analyzing the mood, consider what the writer wants to accomplish and whether the best choice was made to achieve that end.

Analyzing Nuances in Words

Language is not as simple as one word directly correlated to one meaning. Rather, one word can express a vast array of diverse meanings, and similar meanings can be expressed through different words. However, there are very few words that express exactly the same meaning. For this reason, it is important to be able to pick up on the nuances of word meaning.

Many words contain two levels of meaning: connotation and denotation as discussed previously in the informational texts and rhetoric section. A word's *denotation* is its most literal meaning—the definition that can readily be found in the dictionary. A word's *connotation* includes all of its emotional and cultural associations.

In literary writing, authors rely heavily on connotative meaning to create mood and characterization. The following are two descriptions of a rainstorm:

A. The rain slammed against the windowpane, and the wind howled through the fireplace. A pair of hulking oaks next to the house cast eerie shadows as their branches trembled in the wind.

B. The rain pattered against the windowpane, and the wind whistled through the fireplace. A pair of stately oaks next to the house cast curious shadows as their branches swayed in the wind.

Description A paints a creepy picture for readers with strongly emotional words like *slammed*, connoting force and violence. *Howled* connotes pain or wildness, and *eerie* and *trembled* connote fear. Overall, the connotative language in this description serves to inspire fear and anxiety.

However, as can be seen in description B, swapping out a few key words for those with different connotations completely changes the feeling of the passage. *Slammed* is replaced with the more cheerful *pattered*, and *hulking* has been swapped out for *stately*. Both words imply something large, but *hulking* is more intimidating whereas *stately* is more respectable. *Curious* and *swayed* seem more playful than the language used in the earlier description. Although both descriptions represent roughly the same situation, the nuances of the emotional language used throughout the passages create a very different sense for readers.

Selective choice of connotative language can also be extremely impactful in other forms of writing, such as editorials or persuasive texts. Through connotative language, writers reveal their biases and opinions while trying to inspire feelings and actions in readers:

A. Parents won't stop complaining about standardized tests.
B. Parents continue to raise concerns about standardized tests.

Readers should be able to identify the nuance in meaning between these two sentences. The first one carries a more negative feeling, implying that parents are being bothersome or whiny. Readers of the second sentence, though, might come away with the feeling that parents are concerned and involved in their children's education. Again, the aggregate of even subtle cues can combine to give a specific

emotional impression to readers, so from an early age, students should be aware of how language can be used to influence readers' opinions.

Another form of non-literal expression can be found in *figures of speech*. As with connotative language, figures of speech tend to be shared within a cultural group and may be difficult to pick up on for learners outside of that group. In some cases, a figure of speech may be based on the literal denotation of the words it contains, but in other cases, a figure of speech is far removed from its literal meaning. A case in point is *irony*, where what is said is the exact opposite of what is meant:

> The new tax plan is poorly planned, based on faulty economic data, and unable to address the financial struggles of middle class families. Yet legislators remain committed to passing this brilliant proposal.

When the writer refers to the proposal as brilliant, the opposite is implied—the plan is "faulty" and "poorly planned." By using irony, the writer means that the proposal is anything but brilliant by using the word in a non-literal sense.

Another figure of speech is *hyperbole*—extreme exaggeration or overstatement. Statements like, "I love you to the moon and back" or "Let's be friends for a million years" utilize hyperbole to convey a greater depth of emotion, without literally committing oneself to space travel or a life of immortality.

Figures of speech may sometimes use one word in place of another. *Synecdoche*, for example, uses a part of something to refer to its whole. The expression "Don't hurt a hair on her head!" implies protecting more than just an individual hair, but rather her entire body. "The art teacher is training a class of Picassos" uses Picasso, one individual notable artist, to stand in for the entire category of talented artists. Another figure of speech using word replacement is *metonymy*, where a word is replaced with something closely associated to it. For example, news reports may use the word "Washington" to refer to the American government or "the crown" to refer to the British monarch.

Human Language Structures

Nature of Human Language

Language arts educators often seem to be in the position of teaching the "right" way to use English, particularly in lessons about grammar and vocabulary. However, all it takes is back-to-back viewings of speeches by the queen of England and the president of the United States or side-by-side readings of a contemporary poem and one written in the 1600s to come to the conclusion that there is no single, fixed, correct form of spoken or written English. Instead, language varies and evolves across different regions and time periods. It also varies between cultural groups depending on factors such as race, ethnicity, age, and socioeconomic status. Students should come away from a language arts class with more than a strictly prescriptive view of language; they should have an appreciation for its rich diversity.

It is important to understand some key terms in discussing linguistic variety.

Language is a tool for communication. It may be spoken, unspoken—as with body language—written, or codified in other ways. Language is symbolic in the sense that it can describe objects, ideas, and events that are not actually present, have not actually occurred, or only exist in the mind of the speaker. All languages are governed by systematic rules of grammar and semantics. These rules allow speakers to manipulate a finite number of elements, such as sounds or written symbols, to create an infinite number of meanings.

A *dialect* is a distinct variety of a language in terms of patterns of grammar, vocabulary, and/or *phonology*—the sounds used by its speakers—that distinguish it from other forms of that language. Two dialects are not considered separate languages if they are *mutually intelligible*—if speakers of each dialect are able to understand one another. A dialect is not a subordinate version of a language. Examples of English dialects include Scottish English and American Southern English.

By definition, *Standard English* is a dialect. It is one variety of English with its own usage of grammar, vocabulary, and pronunciation. Given that Standard English is taught in schools and used in places like government, journalism, and other professional workplaces, it is often elevated above other English dialects. Linguistically, though, there is nothing that makes Standard English more correct or advanced than other dialects.

A *pidgin* is formed when speakers of different languages begin utilizing a simplified mixture of elements from both languages to communicate with each other. In North America, pidgins occurred when Africans were brought to European colonies as slaves, leading to a mixture of African and European languages. Historically, pidgins also sprung up in areas of international trade. A pidgin is communication born of necessity and lacks the full complexity or standardized rules that govern a language.

When a pidgin becomes widely used and is taught to children as their native language, it becomes a *Creole*. An example is Haitian Creole, a language based on French and including elements of West African languages.

An *accent* is a unique speech pattern, particularly in terms of tone or intonation. Speakers from different regions tend to have different accents, as do learners of English from different native languages. In some cases, accents are mutually intelligible, but in other cases, speakers with different accents might have some difficulty in understanding one another.

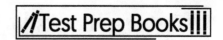

Colloquial language is language that is used conversationally or familiarly—e.g., "What's up?"—in contrast to formal, professional, or academic language—"How are you this evening?"

Vernacular refers to the native, everyday language of a place. Historically, for instance, Bibles and religious services across Europe were primarily offered in Latin, even centuries after the fall of the Roman Empire. After the revolution of the printing press and the widespread availability of vernacular translations of the Bible in the fifteenth and sixteenth centuries, everyday citizens were able to study from Bibles in their own language without needing specialized training in Latin.

A *regionalism* is a word or expression used in a particular region. In the United States, for instance, examples of regionalisms might be *soda*, *pop*, or *Coke*—terms that vary in popularity according to region.

Jargon is vocabulary used within a specialized field, such as computer programming or mechanics. Jargon may consist of specialized words or of everyday words that have a different meaning in this specialized context.

Slang refers to non-standard expressions that are not used in elevated speech and writing. Slang creates linguistic in-groups and out-groups of people, those who can understand the slang terms and those who can't. Slang is often tied to a specific time period. For example, "groovy" and "far out" are connected to the 1970s, and "as if!" and "4-1-1-" are connected to the 1990s.

Understanding Dialect and its Appropriateness

Certain forms of language are viewed differently depending on the context. Lessons learned in the classroom have a real-life application to a student's future, so he or she should know where, when, and how to utilize different forms of language.

Awareness of dialect can help students as readers. Many writers of literary fiction and nonfiction utilize dialect and colloquialisms to add verisimilitude to their writing. This is especially true for authors who focus on a particular region or cultural group in their works, also known as *regionalism* or *local color literature*. Examples include Zora Neale Hurston's *Their Eyes Were Watching God* and the short stories of Kate Chopin. Students can be asked to consider how the speech patterns in a text affect a reader's understanding of the characters—how the pattern reflects a character's background and place in society. They might consider a reader's impression of the region—how similar or different it is from the reader's region or what can be inferred about the region based on how people speak. In some cases, unfamiliar dialect may be very difficult for readers to understand on the page but becomes much more intelligible when read aloud—as in the reading of Shakespeare.

Word Analysis

It is imperative that educators understand the five basic components of reading education. If there is any deficit in any one of these following components, a child is likely to experience reading difficulty:

- Phonemic Awareness
- Phonics
- Fluency
- Vocabulary
- Comprehension

Phonemic Awareness

A phoneme is the smallest unit of sound in a given language and is one aspect under the umbrella of skills associated with phonological awareness. A child demonstrates phonemic awareness when identifying rhymes, recognizing alliterations, and isolating specific sounds inside a word or a set of words. Students who demonstrate basic phonemic awareness will eventually also be able to independently and appropriately blend together a variety of phonemes.

Some classroom strategies to strengthen phonemic awareness may include:

- Introduction to nursery rhymes and word play
- Speech discrimination techniques to train the ear to hear more accurately
- Repeated instruction connecting sounds to letters and blending sounds
- Use of visual images coupled with corresponding sounds and words
- Teaching speech sounds through direct instruction
- Comparing known to unfamiliar words
- Practicing pronunciation of newly introduced letters, letter combinations, and words
- Practicing word decoding
- Differentiating similar sounding words

Inflection Derivation and Compounding

Inflection is the modification of a word to show different grammatical categories such as tense, case, number, and other aspects. This is done by changing a given word's prefix, suffix, or infix to alter the word's meaning. For example, changing the suffix of the word *cling*, you can make it *clung* and *clang*, expressing different cases. It's important to note that inflection retains the original meaning of the word; only the way in which it is used in the sentences changes.

Derivation is when a new prefix or suffix is added to an existing word to create a new word. Unlike inflection, this process actually does change the meaning of the new word. For example, consider when the suffix *ness* is added to the word *slow* to make *slowness*. Both words are connected with slow: not moving fast. However, slowness describes the quality of not moving fast while slow *is* the act of moving without speed. The terms are related but different.

Compounding involves the binding of two or more words to form a single word with a new meaning. The words are usually unrelated but brought together for a specific term such as *footrace* or *sleepwalk*. These new words are called compound words. Compound words can be formed by combining a noun and a verb, like the previous examples, or by combining two nouns like *snowstorm*. Compounds can also be formed using adjectives, adverbs, and propositions. Some compound words utilize a dash to connect the word or phrase such as: *environmentally-friendly*.

Phonological and Phonemic Awareness Instruction

Age-appropriate and developmentally appropriate instruction for phonological and phonemic awareness is key to helping students strengthen their reading and writing skills. Phonological and phonemic awareness, or PPA, instruction works to enhance correct speech, improve understanding and application of accurate letter-to-sound correspondence, and strengthen spelling skills. Since skill-building involving phonemes is not a natural process but needs to be taught, PPA instruction is especially important for students who have limited access and exposure to reading materials and who lack familial encouragement to read. Strategies that educators can implement include leading word and sound

games, focusing on phoneme skill-building activities, and ensuring all activities focus on the fun, playful nature of words and sounds instead of rote memorization and drilling techniques.

Phonics

Phonics is the ability to apply letter-sound relationships and letter patterns in order to accurately pronounce written words. Students with strong phonics skills are able to recognize familiar written words with relative ease and quickly decipher or "decode" unfamiliar words. As one of the foundational skills for reading readiness, phonics essentially enables young readers to translate printed words into recognizable speech. If students lack proficiency in phonics, their ability to read fluently and to increase vocabulary will be limited, which consequently leads to reading comprehension difficulties.

Emergent readers benefit from explicit word decoding instruction that focuses on letter-sound relationships. This includes practicing sounding out words and identifying exceptions to the letter-sound relationships. A multi-sensory approach to word decoding instruction has also been found to be beneficial. By addressing a wide variety of learning styles and providing visual and hands-on instruction, educators help to bridge the gap between guided word decoding and it as an automatic process.

Syntax, Semantics, and Pragmatics

Syntax

With its origins from the Greek word, "syntaxis," which means arrangement, *syntax* is the study of phrase and sentence formation. The study of syntax focuses on the ways in which specific words can be combined to create coherent meaning. For example: the simple rearrangement of the words, "I can run," is different from the question, "Can I run?" which is also different from the meaningless "Run I can."

The following methods can be used to teach syntax:

- Proper Syntax Modeling: Students don't need to be corrected for improper syntax. Instead, they should be shown ways to rephrase what they said with proper syntax. If a student says, "Run I can," then the teacher should say, "Oh, you can run how fast?" This puts syntax in place with conversational skills.

- Open-Ended Sentences: Students can complete open-ended sentences with proper syntax both orally and in written format, or they can correct sentences that have improper syntax so that they make sense.

- Listening for Syntax: Syntax is auditory. Students can often hear a syntax error before they can see it in writing. Teachers should have students use word cards or word magnets to arrange and rearrange simple sentences and read them aloud to check for syntax.

- Repetition: Syntax can be practiced by using songs, poems, and rhymes for repetitive automation.

Semantics

Semantics is the branch of linguistics that addresses meanings. Morphemes, words, phrases, and sentences all carry distinct meanings. The way these individual parts are arranged can have a significant effect on meaning. In order to construct language, students must be able to use semantics to arrange and rearrange words to achieve the particular meaning they are striving for. Activities that teach semantics revolve around teaching the arrangement of word parts (morphology) and root words, and then the teaching of vocabulary. Moving from vocabulary words into studying sentences and sentence structure leads students to learn how to use context clues to determine meaning and to understand anomalies such as metaphors, idioms, and allusions. There are five types of semantic relationships that are critical to understand:

- *Hyponyms* refer to a relationship between words where general words have multiple more-specific words (hyponyms) that fall into the same category (e.g., horse: mare, stallion, foal, Appaloosa, Clydesdale).

- *Meronyms* refer to a relationship between words where a whole word has multiple parts (meronyms) that comprise it (e.g., horse: tail, mane, hooves, ears).

- *Synonyms* refer to words that have the same meaning as another word (e.g., instructor/teacher/educator, canine/dog, feline/cat, herbivore/vegetarian).

- *Antonyms* refer to words that have the opposite meaning as another word (e.g., true/false, up/down, in/out, right/wrong).

- *Homonyms* refer to words that are spelled the same (homographs) or sound the same (homophones) but mean different things (e.g., there/their/they're, two/too/to, principal/principle, plain/plane, (kitchen) sink/ sink (down as in water)).

Pragmatics

Pragmatics is the study of what words mean in certain situations. It helps to understand the intentions and interpretations of intentions through words used in human interaction. Different listeners and different situations call for different language and intonations of language. When people engage in a conversation, it is usually to convey a certain message, and the message (even using the same words) can change depending on the setting and the audience. The more fluent the speaker, the more success she or he will have in conveying the intended message.

The following methods can be used to teach pragmatics:

- When students state something incorrectly, a response can be given to what they intended to say in the first place. For instance, if a student says, "That's how it didn't happen." Then the teacher might say, "Of course, that's not how it happened." Instead of putting students on defense by being corrected, this method puts them at ease and helps them learn.

- Role-playing conversations with different people in different situations can help teach pragmatics. For example, pretend playing can be used where a situation remains the same but the audience changes, or the audience stays the same but the situations change. This can be followed with a discussion about how language and intonations change too.

- Different ways to convey a message can be used, such as asking vs. persuading, or giving direct vs. indirect requests and polite vs. impolite messages.

- Various non-verbal signals can be used to see how they change pragmatics. For example, students can be encouraged to use mismatched words and facial expressions, such as angry words while smiling or happy words while pretending to cry.

Editing and Revising

POWER Strategy

The POWER strategy helps all students to take ownership of the writing process by prompting them to consciously focus on what they are writing.

The POWER strategy is an acronym for the following:

- Prewriting or Planning
- Organizing
- Writing a first draft
- Evaluating the writing
- Revising and rewriting

Prewriting and Planning
During the Prewriting and Planning phase, students learn to consider their audience and purpose for the writing project. Then they compile information they wish to include in the piece of writing from their background knowledge and/or new sources.

Organizing
Next, students decide on the organizational structure of their writing project. There are many types of organizational structures, but the common ones are: story/narrative, informative, opinion, persuasive, compare and contrast, explanatory, and problem/solution formats. Often graphic organizers are an important part of helping students complete this step of the writing process.

Writing
In this step, students write a complete first draft of their project. Educators may begin by using modeled writing to teach this step in the process. It may be helpful for beginning writers to work in small groups or pairs. Verbalizing their thoughts before writing them is also a helpful technique.

Evaluating
In this stage, students reread their writing and note the segments that are particularly strong or need improvement. Then they participate in peer editing. They ask each other questions about the piece. The peers learn to provide feedback and constructive criticism to help the student improve. Scoring rubrics are a helpful tool in this phase to guide students as they edit each other's work.

Revising and Rewriting
Finally, the student incorporates any changes she or he wishes to make based on the evaluating process. Then students rewrite the piece into a final draft and publish it however it best fits the audience and purpose of the writing.

Audience, Purpose, and Context

An author's *writing style*—the way in which words, grammar, punctuation, and sentence fluidity are used—is the most influential element in a piece of writing, and it is dependent on the purpose and the audience for whom it is intended. Together, a writing style and mode of writing form the foundation of a written work, and a good writer will choose the most effective mode and style to convey a message to readers.

Writers should first determine what they are trying to say and then choose the most effective mode of writing to communicate that message. Different writing modes and *word choices* will affect the tone of a piece—that is, its underlying attitude, emotion, or character. The argumentative mode may utilize words that are earnest, angry, passionate, or excited whereas an informative piece may have a sterile, germane, or enthusiastic tone. The tones found in narratives vary greatly, depending on the purpose of the writing. *Tone* will also be affected by the audience—teaching science to children or those who may be uninterested would be most effective with enthusiastic language and exclamation points whereas teaching science to college students may take on a more serious and professional tone, with fewer charged words and punctuation choices that are inherent to academia.

Sentence fluidity—whether sentences are long and rhythmic or short and succinct—also affects a piece of writing as it determines the way in which a piece is read. Children or audiences unfamiliar with a subject do better with short, succinct sentence structures as these break difficult concepts up into shorter points. A period, question mark, or exclamation point is literally a signal for the reader to stop and takes more time to process. Thus, longer, more complex sentences are more appropriate for adults or educated audiences as they can fit more information in between processing time.

The amount of *supporting detail* provided is also tailored to the audience. A text that introduces a new subject to its readers will focus more on broad ideas without going into greater detail whereas a text that focuses on a more specific subject is likely to provide greater detail about the ideas discussed.

Writing styles, like modes, are most effective when tailored to their audiences. Having awareness of an audience's demographic is one of the most crucial aspects of properly communicating an argument, a story, or a set of information.

Text Structures

Writing can be classified under four passage types: narrative, expository, technical, and persuasive. Though these types are not mutually exclusive, one form tends to dominate the rest. By recognizing the *type* of passage you're reading, you gain insight into *how* you should read. If you're reading a narrative, you can assume the author intends to entertain, which means you may skim the text without losing meaning. A technical document might require a close read because skimming the passage might cause the reader to miss salient details.

1. *Narrative* writing, at its core, is the art of storytelling. For a narrative to exist, certain elements must be present. First, it must have characters. While many characters are human, characters could be defined as anything that thinks, acts, and talks like a human. For example, many recent movies, such as *Lord of the Rings* and *The Chronicles of Narnia*, include animals, fantastical creatures, and even trees that behave like humans. Second, it must have a plot or sequence of events. Typically, those events follow a standard plot diagram, but recent trends start *in medias res* or in the middle (near the climax). In this instance, foreshadowing and flashbacks often fill in plot details. Finally, along with characters and a plot, there must also be conflict. Conflict is usually divided into two types: internal and external. Internal conflict indicates the character is in turmoil and is presented through the character's thoughts. External conflicts are visible. Types of external conflict include a person versus nature, another person, or society.

2. *Expository* writing is detached and to the point, while other types of writing—persuasive, narrative, and descriptive—are lively. Since expository writing is designed to instruct or inform, it usually involves directions and steps written in second person ("you" voice) and lacks any persuasive or narrative

elements. Sequence words such as *first*, *second*, and *third*, or *in the first place*, *secondly*, and *lastly* are often given to add fluency and cohesion. Common examples of expository writing include instructor's lessons, cookbook recipes, and repair manuals.

3. Due to its empirical nature, *technical* writing is filled with steps, charts, graphs, data, and statistics. The goal of technical writing is to advance understanding in a field through the scientific method. Experts such as teachers, doctors, or mechanics use words unique to the profession in which they operate. These words, which often incorporate acronyms, are called *jargon*. Technical writing is a type of expository writing but is not meant to be understood by the general public. Instead, technical writers assume readers have received a formal education in a particular field of study and need no explanation as to what the jargon means. Imagine a doctor trying to understand a diagnostic reading for a car or a mechanic trying to interpret lab results. Only professionals with proper training will fully comprehend the text.

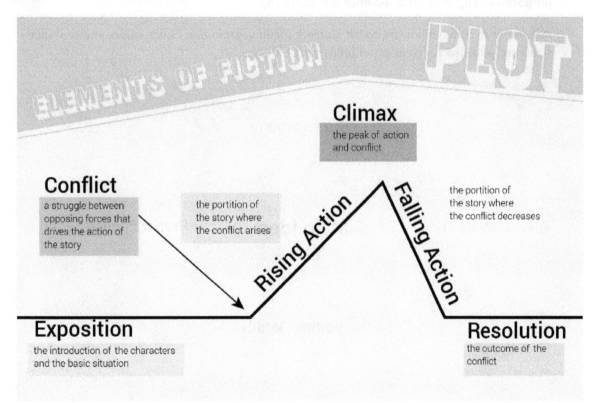

4. *Persuasive* writing is designed to change opinions and attitudes. The topic, stance, and arguments are found in the thesis, positioned near the end of the introduction. Later supporting paragraphs offer relevant quotations, paraphrases, and summaries from primary or secondary sources, which are then interpreted, analyzed, and evaluated. The goal of persuasive writers is not to stack quotes but to develop original ideas by using sources as a starting point. Good persuasive writing makes powerful arguments with valid sources and thoughtful analysis. Poor persuasive writing is riddled with bias and logical fallacies. Sometimes logical and illogical arguments are sandwiched together in the same piece. Therefore, readers should display skepticism when reading persuasive arguments.

<u>Organization of a Text</u>

There are five basic elements inherent in effective writing, and each will be discussed throughout the various subheadings of this section.

- *Main idea*: The driving message of the writing, clearly stated or implied

- *Clear organization*: The effective and purposeful arrangement of the content to support the main idea

- *Supporting details/evidence*: Content that gives appropriate depth and weight to the main idea of the story, argument, or information

- *Diction/tone*: The type of language, vocabulary, and word choice used to express the main idea, purposefully aligned to the audience and purpose

- *Adherence to conventions of English*: Correct spelling, grammar, punctuation, and sentence structure, allowing for clear communication of ideas

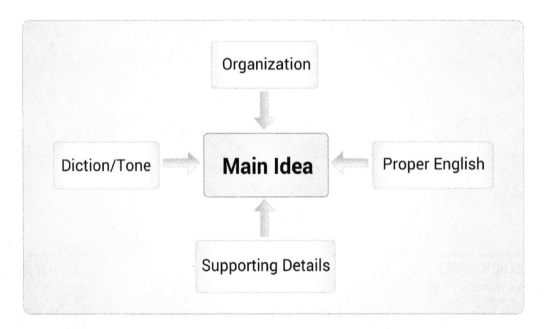

Developing Ideas in an Essay

To distinguish between the common modes of writing, it is important to identify the primary purpose of the work. This can be determined by considering what the author is trying to say to the reader. Although there are countless different styles of writing, all written works tend to fall under four primary categories: argumentative/persuasive, informative expository, descriptive, and narrative.

The table below highlights the purpose, distinct characteristics, and examples of each rhetorical mode.

Writing Mode	Purpose	Distinct Characteristics	Examples
Argumentative	To persuade	Opinions, loaded or subjective language, evidence, suggestions of what the reader should do, calls to action	Critical reviews Political journals Letters of recommendation Cover letters Advertising
Informative	To teach or inform	Objective language, definitions, instructions, factual information	Business and scientific reports Textbooks Instruction manuals News articles Personal letters Wills Informative essays Travel guides Study guides
Descriptive	To deliver sensory details to the reader	Heavy use of adjectives and imagery, language that appeals to any of the five senses	Poetry Journal entries Often used in narrative mode
Narrative	To tell a story, share an experience, entertain	Series of events, plot, characters, dialogue, conflict	Novels Short stories Novellas Anecdotes Biographies Epic poems Autobiographies

Introducing, Developing, and Concluding a Text Effectively

Almost all coherent written works contain three primary parts: a beginning, middle, and end. The organizational arrangements differ widely across distinct writing modes. Persuasive and expository texts utilize an introduction, body, and conclusion whereas narrative works use an orientation, series of events/conflict, and a resolution.

Every element within a written piece relates back to the main idea, and the beginning of a persuasive or expository text generally conveys the main idea or the purpose. For a narrative piece, the beginning is the section that acquaints the reader with the characters and setting, directing them to the purpose of the writing. The main idea in narrative may be implied or addressed at the end of the piece.

Depending on the primary purpose, the arrangement of the middle will adhere to one of the basic organizational structures described in the information texts and rhetoric section. They are cause and effect, problem and solution, compare and contrast, description/spatial, sequence, and order of importance.

The ending of a text is the metaphorical wrap-up of the writing. A solid ending is crucial for effective writing as it ties together loose ends, resolves the action, highlights the main points, or repeats the central idea. A conclusion ensures that readers come away from a text understanding the author's main idea. The table below highlights the important characteristics of each part of a piece of writing.

Structure	Argumentative/Informative	Narrative
Beginning	Introduction *Purpose, main idea*	Orientation *Introduces characters, setting, necessary background*
Middle	Body *Supporting details, reasons and evidence*	Events/Conflict *Story's events that revolve around a central conflict*
End	Conclusion *Highlights main points, summarizes and paraphrases ideas, reiterates the main idea*	Resolution *The solving of the central conflict*

Rhetorical Techniques

In an argument or persuasive text, an author will strive to sway readers to an opinion or conclusion. To be effective, an author must consider his or her intended audience. Although an author may write text for a general audience, he or she will use methods of appeal or persuasion to convince that audience. Aristotle asserted that there were three methods or modes by which a person could be persuaded. These are referred to as *rhetorical appeals*.

The three main types of rhetorical appeals are shown in the following graphic.

Ethos
Credibility of
an author

Rhetoric

Pathos
Emotional
Response

Logos
Logical
Reasoning

Ethos, also referred to as an *ethical appeal*, is an appeal to the audience's perception of the writer as credible (or not), based on their examination of their ethics and who the writer is, his/her experience or incorporation of relevant information, or his/her argument. For example, authors may present testimonials to bolster their arguments. The reader who critically examines the veracity of the testimonials and the credibility of those giving the testimony will be able to determine if the author's use of testimony is valid to his or her argument. In turn, this will help the reader determine if the author's thesis is valid. An author's careful and appropriate use of technical language can create an overall knowledgeable effect and, in turn, act as a convincing vehicle when it comes to credibility. Overuse of technical language, however, may create confusion in readers and obscure an author's overall intent.

Pathos, also referred to as a *pathetic* or *emotional appeal*, is an appeal to the audience's sense of identity, self-interest, or emotions. A critical reader will notice when the author is appealing to pathos through anecdotes and descriptions that elicit an emotion such as anger or pity. Readers should also beware of factual information that uses generalization to appeal to the emotions. While it's tempting to believe an author is the source of truth in his or her text, an author who presents factual information as universally true, consistent throughout time, and common to all groups is using *generalization*. Authors who exclusively use generalizations without specific facts and credible sourcing are attempting to sway readers solely through emotion.

Logos, also referred to as a *logical appeal*, is an appeal to the audience's ability to see and understand the logic in a claim offered by the writer. A critical reader has to be able to evaluate an author's arguments for validity of reasoning and for sufficiency when it comes to argument.

Vocabulary

A writer's style is the way that he or she presents information through sentence structure, word choice, and even punctuation. Style is influenced by the writing situation and the intended audience. A writer's voice is an element of style that shows the writer's personality. It is what makes the writing unique to the writer. Voice and style can be developed through listening to examples of styles in other's writing. Developing an ear for different writing styles can help students to develop their own style.

Precision
People often think of precision in terms of math, but precise word choice is another key to successful writing. Since language itself is imprecise, it's important for the writer to find the exact word or words to convey the full, intended meaning of a given situation. For example:

> The number of deaths has gone down since seat belt laws started.

There are several problems with this sentence. First, the word *deaths* is too general. From the context, it's assumed that the writer is referring only to deaths caused by car accidents. However, without clarification, the sentence lacks impact and is probably untrue. The phrase "gone down" might be accurate, but a more precise word could provide more information and greater accuracy. Did the numbers show a slow and steady decrease of highway fatalities or a sudden drop? If the latter is true, the writer is missing a chance to make their point more dramatically. Instead of "gone down" they could substitute *plummeted, fallen drastically*, or *rapidly diminished* to bring the information to life. Also, the phrase "seat belt laws" is unclear. Does it refer to laws requiring cars to include seat belts or to laws requiring drivers and passengers to use them? Finally, *started* is not a strong verb. Words like *enacted* or *adopted* are more direct and make the content more real. When put together, these changes create a far more powerful sentence:

> The number of highway fatalities has plummeted since laws requiring seat belt usage were enacted.

However, it's important to note that precise word choice can sometimes be taken too far. If the writer of the sentence above takes precision to an extreme, it might result in the following:

> The incidence of high-speed, automobile accident related fatalities has decreased 75% and continued to remain at historical lows since the initial set of federal legislations requiring seat belt use were enacted in 1992.

This sentence is extremely precise, but it takes so long to achieve that precision that it suffers from a lack of clarity. Precise writing is about finding the right balance between information and flow. This is also an issue of conciseness (discussed in the next section).

The last thing to consider with precision is a word choice that's not only unclear or uninteresting, but also confusing or misleading. For example:

> The number of highway fatalities has become hugely lower since laws requiring seat belt use were enacted.

In this case, the reader might be confused by the word *hugely*. Huge means large, but here the writer uses *hugely* to describe something small. Though most readers can decipher this, doing so disconnects them from the flow of the writing and makes the writer's point less effective.

Conciseness

"Less is more" is a good rule to follow when writing a sentence. Unfortunately, writers often include extra words and phrases that seem necessary at the time but add nothing to the main idea. This confuses the reader and creates unnecessary repetition. Writing that lacks conciseness is usually guilty of excessive wordiness and redundant phrases. Here's an example containing both of these issues:

> When legislators decided to begin creating legislation making it mandatory for automobile drivers and passengers to make use of seat belts while in cars, a large number of them made those laws for reasons that were political reasons.

There are several empty or "fluff" words here that take up too much space. These can be eliminated while still maintaining the writer's meaning. For example:

- "Decided to begin" could be shortened to"began"
- "Making it mandatory for" could be shortened to "requiring"
- "Make use of" could be shortened to "use"
- "A large number" could be shortened to "many"

In addition, there are several examples of redundancy that can be eliminated:

- "Legislators decided to begin creating legislation" and "made those laws"
- "Automobile drivers and passengers" and "while in cars"
- "Reasons that were political reasons"

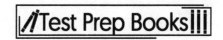

These changes are incorporated as follows:

When legislators began requiring drivers and passengers to use seat belts, many of them did so for political reasons.

There are many general examples of redundant phrases, such as "add an additional," "complete and total," "time schedule," and "transportation vehicle." If asked to identify a redundant phrase on the test, look for words that are close together with the same (or similar) meanings.

Devices to Control Focus

Active and Passive Voice

Active voice is a sentence structure in which the subject performs the action of the sentence. The verbs of these sentences are called *active verbs*.

The deer jumped over the fence.

In the example above, the deer is the one jumping. *Passive voice* is a sentence structure in which the object performs the action of the sentence. The verbs of these sentences are called *passive verbs*.

The fence was jumped by the deer.

In this example, the fence is the subject, but it is not jumping over anything. The deer is still the one performing the action, but it is now the object of the sentence.

Passive voice is helpful when it's unclear who performed an action.

The chair was moved.

While passive voice can add variety to writing, active voice is the generally preferred sentence structure.

Expletives and Concrete Subjects

Controlling the sentence is the art of keeping content direct and targeted. This can be aided by drawing the reader's focus to specific details in the text by avoiding expletives. Expletives are words that unnecessarily take up space and complicate the overall sentence. Here's an example:

Alligators are likely to be inactive in winter.

Cutting out the unnecessary words will make the sentence more direct and increase the flow of the overall paragraph:

Alligators are mostly inactive in winter.

Taking away *are* and *likely to be* streamlines the sentence and makes the main point of the sentence clearer.

Using concrete subjects will also enable the reader to pinpoint what's being talked about. This also personalizes and clarifies the subject matter. Here's an example:

We went to the house.

This is very vague, it can be anyone's house, or it can be anywhere. Therefore, the sentence lacks clarity and control. This is easily remedied with a concrete subject such as:

> We went to Brian's house.

Now the sentence is more direct and the reader is aware of what's going on.

<u>Using Varied and Effective Transitions</u>

Transitions are the glue that holds the writing together. They function to purposefully incorporate new topics and supporting details in a smooth and coherent way. Usually, transitions are found at the beginnings of sentences, but they can also be located in the middle as a way to link clauses together. There are two types of clauses: independent and dependent as discussed in the language use and vocabulary section.

Transition words connect clauses within and between sentences for smoother writing. "I dislike apples. They taste like garbage." is choppier than "I dislike apples because they taste like garbage." Transitions demonstrate the relationship between ideas, allow for more complex sentence structures, and can alert the reader to which type of organizational format the author is using.

Transition words can be categorized based on the relationships they create between ideas:

- General order: signaling elaboration of an idea to emphasize a point—e.g., for example, for instance, to demonstrate, including, such as, in other words, that is, in fact, also, furthermore, likewise, and, truly, so, surely, certainly, obviously, doubtless

- Chronological order: referencing the time frame in which main event or idea occurs—e.g., before, after, first, while, soon, shortly thereafter, meanwhile

- Numerical order/order of importance: indicating that related ideas, supporting details, or events will be described in a sequence, possibly in order of importance—e.g., first, second, also, finally, another, in addition, equally important, less importantly, most significantly, the main reason, last but not least

- Spatial order: referring to the space and location of something or where things are located in relation to each other—e.g., inside, outside, above, below, within, close, under, over, far, next to, adjacent to

- Cause and effect order: signaling a causal relationship between events or ideas—e.g., thus, therefore, since, resulted in, for this reason, as a result, consequently, hence, for, so

- Compare and contrast order: identifying the similarities and differences between two or more objects, ideas, or lines of thought—e.g., like, as, similarly, equally, just as, unlike, however, but, although, conversely, on the other hand, on the contrary

- Summary order: indicating that a particular idea is coming to a close—e.g., in conclusion, to sum up, in other words, ultimately, above all

Sophisticated writing also aims to avoid overuse of transitions and ensure that those used are meaningful. Using a variety of transitions makes the writing appear more lively and informed and helps readers follow the progression of ideas.

Practice Test #1

Questions 1–9 are based on the following passage:

While all dogs (1) descend through gray wolves, it's easy to notice that dog breeds come in a variety of shapes and sizes. With such a (2) drastic range of traits, appearances and body types dogs are one of the most variable and adaptable species on the planet. (3) But why so many differences. The answer is that humans have actually played a major role in altering the biology of dogs. (4) This was done through a process called selective breeding.

(5) Selective breeding which is also called artificial selection is the processes in which animals with desired traits are bred in order to produce offspring that share the same traits. In natural selection, (6) animals must adapt to their environments increase their chance of survival. Over time, certain traits develop in animals that enable them to thrive in these environments. Those animals with more of these traits, or better versions of these traits, gain an (7) advantage over others of their species. Therefore, the animal's chances to mate are increased and these useful (8) genes are passed into their offspring. With dog breeding, humans select traits that are desired and encourage more of these desired traits in other dogs by breeding dogs that already have them.

The reason for different breeds of dogs is that there were specific needs that humans wanted to fill with their animals. For example, scent hounds are known for their extraordinary ability to track game through scent. These breeds are also known for their endurance in seeking deer and other prey. Therefore, early hunters took dogs that displayed these abilities and bred them to encourage these traits. Later, these generations took on characteristics that aided these desired traits. (9) For example, Bloodhounds have broad snouts and droopy ears that fall to the ground when they smell. These physical qualities not only define the look of the Bloodhound, but also contribute to their amazing tracking ability. The broad snout is able to define and hold onto scents longer than many other breeds. The long, floppy ears serve to collect and hold the scents the earth holds so that the smells are clearer and able to be distinguished.

1. Which of the following would be the best choice for this sentence (reproduced below)?

While all dogs (1) descend through gray wolves, it's easy to notice that dog breeds come in a variety of shapes and sizes.

a. NO CHANGE
b. descend by gray wolves
c. descend from gray wolves
d. descended through gray wolves

2. Which of the following would be the best choice for this sentence (reproduced below)?

With such a (2) <u>drastic range of traits, appearances and body types</u>, dogs are one of the most variable and adaptable species on the planet.

a. NO CHANGE
b. drastic range of traits, appearances, and body types,
c. drastic range of traits and appearances and body types,
d. drastic range of traits, appearances, as well as body types,

3. Which of the following would be the best choice for this sentence (reproduced below)?

(3) <u>But why so many differences.</u>

a. NO CHANGE
b. But are there so many differences?
c. But why so many differences are there.
d. But why so many differences?

4. Which of the following would be the best choice for this sentence (reproduced below)?

(4) <u>This was done through a process called selective breeding.</u>

a. NO CHANGE
b. This was done, through a process called selective breeding.
c. This was done, through a process, called selective breeding.
d. This was done through selective breeding, a process.

5. Which of the following would be the best choice for this sentence (reproduced below)?

(5) <u>Selective breeding which is also called artificial selection is the processes</u> in which animals with desired traits are bred in order to produce offspring that share the same traits.

a. NO CHANGE
b. Selective breeding, which is also called artificial selection is the processes
c. Selective breeding which is also called, artificial selection, is the processes
d. Selective breeding, which is also called artificial selection, is the processes

6. Which of the following would be the best choice for this sentence (reproduced below)?

In natural selection, (6) <u>animals must adapt to their environments increase their chance of survival.</u>

a. NO CHANGE
b. animals must adapt to their environments to increase their chance of survival.
c. animals must adapt to their environments, increase their chance of survival.
d. animals must adapt to their environments, increasing their chance of survival.

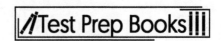

7. Which of the following would be the best choice for this sentence (reproduced below)?

Those animals with more of these traits, or better versions of these traits, gain an (7) <u>advantage over others of their species.</u>

a. NO CHANGE
b. advantage over others, of their species.
c. advantages over others of their species.
d. advantage over others.

8. Which of the following would be the best choice for this sentence (reproduced below)?

Therefore, the animal's chances to mate are increased and these useful (8) <u>genes are passed into their offspring.</u>

a. NO CHANGE
b. genes are passed onto their offspring.
c. genes are passed on to their offspring.
d. genes are passed within their offspring.

9. Which of the following would be the best choice for this sentence (reproduced below)?

(9) <u>For example, Bloodhounds</u> have broad snouts and droopy ears that fall to the ground when they smell.

a. NO CHANGE
b. For example, Bloodhounds,
c. For example Bloodhounds
d. For example, bloodhounds

Questions 10–18 are based on the following passage:

I'm not alone when I say that it's hard to pay attention sometimes. I can't count how many times I've sat in a classroom, lecture, speech, or workshop and (10) <u>been bored to tears or rather sleep</u>. (11) <u>Usually I turn to doodling in order to keep awake</u>. This never really helps; I'm not much of an artist. Therefore, after giving up on drawing a masterpiece, I would just concentrate on keeping my eyes open and trying to be attentive. This didn't always work because I wasn't engaged in what was going on.

(12) <u>Sometimes in particularly dull seminars,</u> I'd imagine comical things going on in the room or with the people trapped in the room with me. Why? (13) <u>Because I wasn't invested in what was going on I wasn't motivated to listen.</u> I'm not going to write about how I conquered the difficult task of actually paying attention in a difficult or unappealing class—it can be done, sure. I have sat through the very epitome of boredom (in my view at least) several times and come away learning something. (14) <u>Everyone probably has had to at one time do this</u>. What I want to talk about is that profound moment when curiosity is sparked (15) <u>in another person drawing them to pay attention to what is before them</u> and expand their knowledge.

What really makes people pay attention? (16) <u>Easy it's interest</u>. This doesn't necessarily mean (17) <u>embellishing subject matter drawing people's attention.</u> This won't always work. However, an individual can present material in a way that is clear to understand and actually engages the audience. Asking questions to the audience or class will make them a part of the topic at hand. Discussions that make people think about the content and (18) how it applies to there lives world and future is key. If math is being discussed, an instructor can explain the purpose behind the equations or perhaps use real-world applications to show how relevant the topic is. When discussing history, a lecturer can prompt students to imagine themselves in the place of key figures and ask how they might respond. The bottom line is to explore the ideas rather than just lecture. Give people the chance to explore material from multiple angles, and they'll be hungry to keep paying attention for more information.

10. Which of the following would be the best choice for this sentence (reproduced below)?

I can't count how many times I've sat in a classroom, lecture, speech, or workshop and (10) been bored to tears or rather sleep.

a. NO CHANGE
b. been bored to, tears, or rather sleep.
c. been bored, to tears or rather sleep.
d. been bored to tears or, rather, sleep.

11. Which of the following would be the best choice for this sentence (reproduced below)?

(11) Usually I turn to doodling in order to keep awake.

a. NO CHANGE
b. Usually, I turn to doodling in order to keep awake.
c. Usually I turn to doodling, in order, to keep awake.
d. Usually I turned to doodling in order to keep awake.

12. Which of the following would be the best choice for this sentence (reproduced below)?

(12) Sometimes in particularly dull seminars, I'd imagine comical things going on in the room or with the people trapped in the room with me.

a. NO CHANGE
b. Sometimes, in particularly, dull seminars,
c. Sometimes in particularly dull seminars
d. Sometimes in particularly, dull seminars,

13. Which of the following would be the best choice for this sentence (reproduced below)?

(13) Because I wasn't invested in what was going on I wasn't motivated to listen.

a. NO CHANGE
b. Because I wasn't invested, in what was going on, I wasn't motivated to listen.
c. Because I wasn't invested in what was going on. I wasn't motivated to listen.
d. I wasn't motivated to listen because I wasn't invested in what was going on.

14. Which of the following would be the best choice for this sentence (reproduced below)?

(14) Everyone probably has had to at one time do this.

a. NO CHANGE
b. Everyone probably has had to, at one time. Do this.
c. Everyone's probably had to do this at some time.
d. At one time everyone probably has had to do this.

15. Which of the following would be the best choice for this sentence (reproduced below)?

What I want to talk about is that profound moment when curiosity is sparked (15) in another person drawing them to pay attention to what is before them and expand their knowledge.

a. NO CHANGE
b. in another person, drawing them to pay attention
c. in another person; drawing them to pay attention to what is before them.
d. in another person, drawing them to pay attention to what is before them.

16. Which of the following would be the best choice for this sentence (reproduced below)?

(16) Easy it's interest.

a. NO CHANGE
b. Easy it is interest.
c. Easy. It's interest.
d. Easy—it's interest.

17. Which of the following would be the best choice for this sentence (reproduced below)?

This doesn't necessarily mean (17) embellishing subject matter drawing people's attention.

a. NO CHANGE
b. embellishing subject matter which draws people's attention.
c. embellishing subject matter to draw people's attention.
d. embellishing subject matter for the purpose of drawing people's attention.

18. Which of the following would be the best choice for this sentence (reproduced below)?

Discussions that make people think about the content and (18) how it applies to there lives world and future is key.

a. NO CHANGE
b. how it applies to their lives, world, and future is key.
c. how it applied to there lives world and future is key.
d. how it applies to their lives, world and future is key.

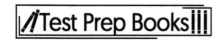

Questions 19–27 are based on the following passage:

Since the first discovery of dinosaur bones, (19) <u>scientists has made strides in technological development and methodologies used to investigate</u> these extinct animals. We know more about dinosaurs than ever before and are still learning fascinating new things about how they looked and lived. However, one has to ask, (20) <u>how if earlier perceptions of dinosaurs</u> continue to influence people's understanding of these creatures? Can these perceptions inhibit progress towards further understanding of dinosaurs?

(21) <u>The biggest problem with studying dinosaurs is simply that there are no living dinosaurs to observe.</u> All discoveries associated with these animals are based on physical remains. To gauge behavioral characteristics, scientists cross-examine these (22) <u>finds with living animals that seem similar in order to gain understanding.</u> While this method is effective, these are still deductions. Some ideas about dinosaurs can't be tested and confirmed simply because humans can't replicate a living dinosaur. For example, a Spinosaurus has a large sail, or a finlike structure that grows from its back. Paleontologists know this sail exists and have ideas for the function of (23) <u>the sail however they are uncertain of which idea is the true function.</u> Some scientists believe (24) <u>the sail serves to regulate the Spinosaurus' body temperature and yet others believe its used to attract mates.</u> Still, other scientists think the sail is used to intimidate other predatory dinosaurs for self-defense. These are all viable explanations, but they are also influenced by what scientists know about modern animals. (25) <u>Yet, it's quite possible</u> that the sail could hold a completely unique function.

While it's (26) <u>plausible, even likely that dinosaurs share many</u> traits with modern animals, there is the danger of overattributing these qualities to a unique, extinct species. For much of the early nineteenth century, when people first started studying dinosaur bones, the assumption was that they were simply giant lizards. (27) <u>For the longest time this image was the prevailing view on dinosaurs,</u> until evidence indicated that they were more likely warm blooded. Scientists have also discovered that many dinosaurs had feathers and actually share many traits with modern birds.

19. Which of the following would be the best choice for this sentence (reproduced below)?

Since the first discovery of dinosaur bones, (19) <u>scientists has made strides in technological development and methodologies used to investigate</u> these extinct animals.

a. NO CHANGE
b. scientists has made strides in technological development, and methodologies, used to investigate
c. scientists have made strides in technological development and methodologies used to investigate
d. scientists, have made strides in technological development and methodologies used, to investigate

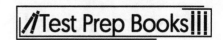

20. Which of the following would be the best choice for this sentence (reproduced below)?

However, one has to ask, (20) how if earlier perceptions of dinosaurs continue to influence people's understanding of these creatures?

a. NO CHANGE
b. how perceptions of dinosaurs
c. how, if, earlier perceptions of dinosaurs
d. whether earlier perceptions of dinosaurs

21. Which of the following would be the best choice for this sentence (reproduced below)?

(21) The biggest problem with studying dinosaurs is simply that there are no living dinosaurs to observe.

a. NO CHANGE
b. The biggest problem with studying dinosaurs is simple, that there are no living dinosaurs to observe.
c. The biggest problem with studying dinosaurs is simple. There are no living dinosaurs to observe.
d. The biggest problem with studying dinosaurs, is simply that there are no living dinosaurs to observe.

22. Which of the following would be the best choice for this sentence (reproduced below)?

To gauge behavioral characteristics, scientists cross-examine these (22) finds with living animals that seem similar in order to gain understanding.

a. NO CHANGE
b. finds with living animals to explore potential similarities.
c. finds with living animals to gain understanding of similarities.
d. finds with living animals that seem similar, in order, to gain understanding.

23. Which of the following would be the best choice for this sentence (reproduced below)?

Paleontologists know this sail exists and have ideas for the function of (23) the sail however they are uncertain of which idea is the true function.

a. NO CHANGE
b. the sail however, they are uncertain of which idea is the true function.
c. the sail however they are, uncertain, of which idea is the true function.
d. the sail; however, they are uncertain of which idea is the true function.

24. Which of the following would be the best choice for this sentence (reproduced below)?

Some scientists believe (24) the sail serves to regulate the Spinosaurus' body temperature and yet others believe its used to attract mates.

a. NO CHANGE
b. the sail serves to regulate the Spinosaurus' body temperature, yet others believe it's used to attract mates.
c. the sail serves to regulate the Spinosaurus' body temperature and yet others believe it's used to attract mates.
d. the sail serves to regulate the Spinosaurus' body temperature however others believe it's used to attract mates.

25. Which of the following would be the best choice for this sentence (reproduced below)?

(25) Yet, it's quite possible that the sail could hold a completely unique function.

a. NO CHANGE
b. Yet, it's quite possible,
c. It's quite possible,
d. Its quite possible

26. Which of the following would be the best choice for this sentence (reproduced below)?

While it's (26) plausible, even likely that dinosaurs share many traits with modern animals, there is the danger of over attributing these qualities to a unique, extinct species.

a. NO CHANGE
b. plausible, even likely that, dinosaurs share many
c. plausible, even likely, that dinosaurs share many
d. plausible even likely that dinosaurs share many

27. Which of the following would be the best choice for this sentence (reproduced below)?

(27) For the longest time this image was the prevailing view on dinosaurs, until evidence indicated that they were more likely warm blooded.

a. NO CHANGE
b. For the longest time this was the prevailing view on dinosaurs
c. For the longest time, this image, was the prevailing view on dinosaurs
d. For the longest time this was the prevailing image of dinosaurs

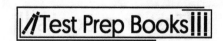

Questions 28–36 are based on the following passage:

Everyone has heard the (28) <u>idea of the end justifying the means; that would be Weston's philosophy</u>. Weston is willing to cross any line, commit any act no matter how heinous, to achieve success in his goal. (29) <u>Ransom is reviled by this fact, seeing total evil in Weston's plan.</u> To do an evil act in order (30) <u>to gain a result that's supposedly good would ultimately warp the final act.</u> (31) <u>This opposing viewpoints immediately distinguishes Ransom as the hero.</u> In the conflict with Un-man, Ransom remains true to his moral principles, someone who refuses to be compromised by power. Instead, Ransom makes it clear that by allowing such processes as murder and lying dictate how one attains a positive outcome, (32) <u>the righteous goal becomes corrupted.</u> The good end would not be truly good, but a twisted end that conceals corrupt deeds.

(33) <u>This idea of allowing necessary evils to happen, is very tempting, it is what Weston fell prey to.</u> (34) <u>The temptation of the evil spirit Un-man ultimately takes over Weston and he is possessed.</u> However, Ransom does not give into temptation. He remains faithful to the truth of what is right and incorrect. This leads him to directly face Un-man for the fate of Perelandra and its inhabitants.

Just as Weston was corrupted by the Un-man, (35) <u>Un-man after this seeks to tempt the Queen of Perelandra </u>to darkness. Ransom must literally (36) <u>show her the right path, to accomplish this, he does this based on the same principle as the "means to an end" argument</u>—that good follows good, and evil follows evil. Later in the plot, Weston/Un-man seeks to use deceptive reasoning to turn the queen to sin, pushing the queen to essentially ignore Melildil's rule to satisfy her own curiosity. In this sense, Un-man takes on the role of a false prophet, a tempter. Ransom must shed light on the truth, but this is difficult; his adversary is very clever and uses brilliant language. Ransom's lack of refinement heightens the weight of Un-man's corrupted logic, and so the Queen herself is intrigued by his logic.

Based on an excerpt from *Perelandra* by C.S. Lewis

28. Which of the following would be the best choice for this sentence (reproduced below)?

Everyone has heard the (28) <u>idea of the end justifying the means; that would be Weston's philosophy.</u>

a. NO CHANGE
b. idea of the end justifying the means; this is Weston's philosophy.
c. idea of the end justifying the means, this is the philosophy of Weston
d. idea of the end justifying the means. That would be Weston's philosophy.

29. Which of the following would be the best choice for this sentence (reproduced below)?

(29) <u>Ransom is reviled by this fact, seeing total evil in Weston's plan.</u>

a. NO CHANGE
b. Ransom is reviled by this fact; seeing total evil in Weston's plan.
c. Ransom, is reviled by this fact, seeing total evil in Weston's plan.
d. Ransom reviled by this, sees total evil in Weston's plan.

30. Which of the following would be the best choice for this sentence (reproduced below)?

To do an evil act in order (30) <u>to gain a result that's supposedly good would ultimately warp the final act.</u>

a. NO CHANGE
b. for an outcome that's for a greater good would ultimately warp the final act.
c. to gain a final act would warp its goodness.
d. to achieve a positive outcome would ultimately warp the goodness of the final act.

31. Which of the following would be the best choice for this sentence (reproduced below)?

(31) <u>This opposing viewpoints immediately distinguishes Ransom as the hero.</u>

a. NO CHANGE
b. This opposing viewpoints immediately distinguishes Ransom, as the hero.
c. This opposing viewpoint immediately distinguishes Ransom as the hero.
d. Those opposing viewpoints immediately distinguishes Ransom as the hero.

32. Which of the following would be the best choice for this sentence (reproduced below)?

Instead, Ransom makes it clear that by allowing such processes as murder and lying dictate how one attains a positive outcome, (32) <u>the righteous goal becomes corrupted.</u>

a. NO CHANGE
b. the goal becomes corrupted and no longer righteous.
c. the righteous goal becomes, corrupted.
d. the goal becomes corrupted, when once it was righteous.

33. Which of the following would be the best choice for this sentence (reproduced below)?

(33) <u>This idea of allowing necessary evils to happen, is very tempting, it is what Weston fell prey to.</u>

a. NO CHANGE
b. This idea of allowing necessary evils to happen, is very tempting. This is what Weston fell prey to.
c. This idea, allowing necessary evils to happen, is very tempting, it is what Weston fell prey to.
d. This tempting idea of allowing necessary evils to happen is what Weston fell prey to.

34. Which of the following would be the best choice for this sentence (reproduced below)?

(34) <u>The temptation of the evil spirit Un-man ultimately takes over Weston and he is possessed.</u>

a. NO CHANGE
b. The temptation of the evil spirit Un-man ultimately takes over and possesses Weston.
c. Weston is possessed as a result of the temptation of the evil spirit Un-man ultimately, who takes over.
d. The temptation of the evil spirit Un-man takes over Weston and he is possessed ultimately.

35. Which of the following would be the best choice for this sentence (reproduced below)?

Just as Weston was corrupted by the Un-man, (35) <u>Un-man after this seeks to tempt the Queen of Perelandra</u> to darkness.

a. NO CHANGE
b. Un-man, after this, would tempt the Queen of Perelandra
c. Un-man, after this, seeks to tempt the Queen of Perelandra
d. Un-man then seeks to tempt the Queen of Perelandra

36. Which of the following would be the best choice for this sentence (reproduced below)?

Ransom must literally (36) <u>show her the right path, to accomplish this, he does this based on the same principle as the "means to an end" argument</u>—that good follows good, and evil follows evil.

a. NO CHANGE
b. show her the right path. To accomplish this, he uses the same principle as the "means to an end" argument
c. show her the right path; to accomplish this he uses the same principle as the "means to an end" argument
d. show her the right path, to accomplish this, the same principle as the "means to an end" argument is applied

Questions 37–45 are based on the following passage:

(37) <u>What's clear about the news is today is that the broader the media</u> the more ways there are to tell a story. Even if different news groups cover the same story, individual newsrooms can interpret or depict the story differently than other counterparts. Stories can also change depending on the type of (38) <u>media in question incorporating different styles and unique</u> ways to approach the news. (39) <u>It is because of these respective media types that ethical and news-related subject matter can sometimes seem different or altered.</u> But how does this affect the narrative of the new story?

I began by investigating a written newspaper article from the Baltimore Sun. Instantly striking are the bolded headlines. (40) <u>These are clearly meant for direct the viewer</u> to the most exciting and important stories the paper has to offer. What was particularly noteworthy about this edition was that the first page dealt with two major ethical issues. (41) <u>On a national level there was a story</u> on the evolving Petraeus scandal involving his supposed affair. The other article was focused locally in Baltimore, a piece questioning the city's Ethics Board and their current director. Just as a television newscaster communicates the story through camera and dialogue, the printed article applies intentional and targeted written narrative style. More so than any of the mediums, a news article seems to be focused specifically on a given story without need to jump to another. Finer details are usually expanded on (42) <u>in written articles, usually people who</u> read newspapers or go online for web articles want more than a quick blurb. The diction of the story is also more precise and can be either straightforward or suggestive (43) <u>depending in earnest on the goal of the writer.</u> However, there's still plenty of room for opinions to be inserted into the text.

Usually, all news (44) <u>outlets have some sort of bias, it's just a question of how much</u> bias clouds the reporting. As long as this bias doesn't withhold information from the reader, it can be considered credible. (45) <u>However an over use of bias,</u> opinion, and suggestive language can rob readers of the chance to interpret the news events for themselves.

37. Which of the following would be the best choice for this sentence (reproduced below)?

(37) <u>What's clear about the news today is that the broader the media</u> the more ways there are to tell a story.

a. NO CHANGE
b. What's clear, about the news today, is that the broader the media
c. What's clear about today's news is that the broader the media
d. The news today is broader than earlier media

38. Which of the following would be the best choice for this sentence (reproduced below)?

Stories can also change depending on the type of (38) <u>media in question incorporating different styles and unique</u> ways to approach the news.

a. NO CHANGE
b. media in question; each incorporates unique styles and unique
c. media in question. To incorporate different styles and unique
d. media in question, incorporating different styles and unique

39. Which of the following would be the best choice for this sentence (reproduced below)?

(39) <u>It is because of these respective media types that ethical and news-related subject matter can sometimes seem different or altered.</u>

a. NO CHANGE
b. It is because of these respective media types, that ethical and news-related subject matter, can sometimes seem different or altered.
c. It is because of these respective media types, that ethical and news-related subject matter can sometimes seem different or altered.
d. It is because of these respective media types that ethical and news-related subject matter can sometimes seem different. Or altered.

40. Which of the following would be the best choice for this sentence (reproduced below)?

(40) <u>These are clearly meant for direct the viewer</u> to the most exciting and important stories the paper has to offer.

a. NO CHANGE
b. These are clearly meant for the purpose of giving direction to the viewer
c. These are clearly meant to direct the viewer
d. These are clearly meant for the viewer to be directed

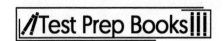

41. Which of the following would be the best choice for this sentence (reproduced below)?

(41) <u>On a national level there was a story</u> on the evolving Petraeus scandal involving his supposed affair.

a. NO CHANGE
b. On a national level a story was there
c. On a national level; there was a story
d. On a national level, there was a story

42. Which of the following would be the best choice for this sentence (reproduced below)?

Finer details are usually expanded on (42) <u>in written articles, usually people who</u> read newspapers or go online for web articles want more than a quick blurb.

a. NO CHANGE
b. in written articles. People who usually
c. in written articles, usually, people who
d. in written articles usually people who

43. Which of the following would be the best choice for this sentence (reproduced below)?

The diction of the story is also more precise and can be either straightforward or suggestive (43) <u>depending in earnest on the goal of the writer.</u>

a. NO CHANGE
b. depending; in earnest on the goal of the writer.
c. depending, in earnest, on the goal of the writer.
d. the goal of the writer, in earnest, depends on the goal of the writer.

44. Which of the following would be the best choice for this sentence (reproduced below)?

Usually, all news (44) <u>outlets have some sort of bias, it's just a question of how much</u> bias clouds the reporting.

a. NO CHANGE
b. outlets have some sort of bias. Just a question of how much
c. outlets have some sort of bias it can just be a question of how much
d. outlets have some sort of bias, its just a question of how much

45. Which of the following would be the best choice for this sentence (reproduced below)?

(45) <u>However an over use of bias,</u> opinion, and suggestive language can rob readers of the chance to interpret the news events for themselves.

a. NO CHANGE
b. However, an over use of bias,
c. However, with too much bias,
d. However, an overuse of bias,

Answer Explanations #1

1. C: Choice *C* correctly uses *from* to describe the fact that dogs are related to wolves. The word *through* is incorrectly used here, so Choice *A* is incorrect. Choice *B* makes no sense. Choice *D* unnecessarily changes the verb tense in addition to incorrectly using *through*.

2. B: Choice *B* is correct because the Oxford comma is applied, clearly separating the specific terms. Choice *A* lacks this clarity. Choice *C* is correct but too wordy since commas can be easily applied. Choice *D* doesn't flow with the sentence's structure.

3. D: Choice *D* correctly uses the question mark, fixing the sentence's main issue. Thus, Choice *A* is incorrect because questions do not end with periods. Choice *B*, although correctly written, changes the meaning of the original sentence. Choice *C* is incorrect because it completely changes the direction of the sentence, disrupts the flow of the paragraph, and lacks the crucial question mark.

4. A: Choice *A* is correct since there are no errors in the sentence. Choices *B* and *C* both have extraneous commas, disrupting the flow of the sentence. Choice *D* unnecessarily rearranges the sentence.

5. D: Choice *D* is correct because the commas serve to distinguish that *artificial selection* is just another term for *selective breeding* before the sentence continues. The structure is preserved, and the sentence can flow with more clarity. Choice *A* is incorrect because the sentence needs commas to avoid being a run-on. Choice *B* is close but still lacks the required comma after *selection*, so this is incorrect. Choice *C* is incorrect because the comma to set off the aside should be placed after *breeding* instead of *called*.

6. B: Choice *B* is correct because the sentence is talking about a continuing process. Therefore, the best modification is to add the word *to* in front of *increase*. Choice *A* is incorrect because this modifier is missing. Choice *C* is incorrect because, with the additional comma, the present tense of *increase* is inappropriate. Choice *D* makes more sense, but the tense is still not the best to use.

7. A: The sentence has no errors, so Choice *A* is correct. Choice *B* is incorrect because it adds an unnecessary comma. Choice *C* is incorrect because *advantage* should not be plural in this sentence without the removal of the singular *an*. Choice *D* is very tempting. While this would make the sentence more concise, this would ultimately alter the context of the sentence, which would be incorrect.

8. C: Choice *C* correctly uses *on to*, describing the way genes are passed generationally. The use of *into* is inappropriate for this context, which makes Choice *A* incorrect. Choice *B* is close, but *onto* refers to something being placed on a surface. Choice *D* doesn't make logical sense.

9. D: Choice *D* is correct, since only proper names should be capitalized. Because the name of a dog breed is not a proper name, Choice *A* is incorrect. In terms of punctuation, only one comma after *example* is needed, so Choices *B* and *C* are incorrect.

10. D: Choice *D* is the correct answer because "rather" acts as an interrupting word here and thus should be separated by commas. Choices *B* and *C* all use commas unwisely, breaking the flow of the sentence.

11. B: Since the sentence can stand on its own without *Usually*, separating it from the rest of the sentence with a comma is correct. Choice *A* needs the comma after *Usually*, while Choice *C* uses

commas incorrectly. Choice *D* is tempting but changing *turn* to past tense goes against the rest of the paragraph.

12. A: In Choice *A*, the dependent clause *Sometimes in particularly dull seminars* is seamlessly attached with a single comma after *seminars*. Choice *B* contains too many commas. Choice *C* does not correctly combine the dependent clause with the independent clause. Choice *D* introduces too many unnecessary commas.

13. D: Choice *D* rearranges the sentence to be more direct and straightforward, so it is correct. Choice *A* needs a comma after *on*. Choice *B* introduces unnecessary commas. Choice *C* creates an incomplete sentence, since *Because I wasn't invested in what was going on* is a dependent clause.

14. C: Choice *C* is fluid and direct, making it the best revision. Choice *A* is incorrect because the construction is awkward and lacks parallel structure. Choice *B* is incorrect because of the unnecessary comma and period. Choice *D* is close, but its sequence is still awkward and overly complicated.

15. B: Choice *B* correctly adds a comma after *person* and cuts out the extraneous writing, making the sentence more streamlined. Choice *A* is poorly constructed, lacking proper grammar to connect the sections of the sentence correctly. Choice *C* inserts an unnecessary semicolon and doesn't enable this section to flow well with the rest of the sentence. Choice *D* is better but still unnecessarily long.

16. D: This sentence, though short, is a complete sentence. The only thing the sentence needs is an em-dash after "Easy." In this sentence the em-dash works to add emphasis to the word "Easy" and also acts in place of a colon, but in a less formal way. Therefore, Choice *D* is correct. Choices *A* and *B* lack the crucial comma, while Choice *C* unnecessarily breaks the sentence apart.

17. C: Choice *C* successfully fixes the construction of the sentence, changing *drawing* into *to draw*. Keeping the original sentence disrupts the flow, so Choice *A* is incorrect. Choice *B*'s use of *which* offsets the whole sentence. Choice *D* is incorrect because it unnecessarily expands the sentence content and makes it more confusing.

18. B: Choice *B* fixes the homophone issue. Because the author is talking about people, *their* must be used instead of *there*. This revision also appropriately uses the Oxford comma, separating and distinguishing *lives, world, and future*. Choice *A* uses the wrong homophone and is missing commas. Choice *C* neglects to fix these problems and unnecessarily changes the tense of *applies*. Choice *D* fixes the homophone but fails to properly separate *world* and *future*.

19. C: Choice *C* is correct because it fixes the core issue with this sentence: the singular *has* should not describe the plural *scientists*. Thus, Choice *A* is incorrect. Choices *B* and *D* add unnecessary commas.

20. D: Choice *D* correctly conveys the writer's intention of asking if, or *whether*, early perceptions of dinosaurs are still influencing people. Choice *A* makes no sense as worded. Choice *B* is better, but *how* doesn't coincide with the context. Choice *C* adds unnecessary commas.

21. A: Choice *A* is correct, as the sentence does not require modification. Choices *B* and *C* implement extra punctuation unnecessarily, disrupting the flow of the sentence. Choice *D* incorrectly adds a comma in an awkward location.

22. B: Choice *B* is the strongest revision, as adding *to explore* is very effective in both shortening the sentence and maintaining, even enhancing, the point of the writer. To explore is to seek understanding in order to gain knowledge and insight, which coincides with the focus of the overall sentence. Choice *A* is not technically incorrect, but it is overcomplicated. Choice *C* is a decent revision, but the sentence could still be more condensed and sharpened. Choice *D* fails to make the sentence more concise and inserts unnecessary commas.

23. D: Choice *D* correctly applies a semicolon to introduce a new line of thought while remaining in a single sentence. The comma after *however* is also appropriately placed. Choice *A* is a run-on sentence. Choice *B* is also incorrect because the single comma is not enough to fix the sentence. Choice *C* adds commas around *uncertain* which are unnecessary.

24. B: Choice *B* not only fixes the homophone issue from *its*, which is possessive, to *it's*, which is a contraction of *it is*, but also streamlines the sentence by adding a comma and eliminating *and*. Choice *A* is incorrect because of these errors. Choices *C* and *D* only fix the homophone issue.

25. A: Choice *A* is correct, as the sentence is fine the way it is. Choices *B* and *C* add unnecessary commas, while Choice *D* uses the possessive *its* instead of the contraction *it's*.

26. C: Choice *C* is correct because the phrase *even likely* is flanked by commas, creating a kind of aside, which allows the reader to see this separate thought while acknowledging it as part of the overall sentence and subject at hand. Choice *A* is incorrect because it seems to ramble after *even* due to a missing comma after *likely*. Choice *B* is better but inserting a comma after *that* warps the flow of the writing. Choice *D* is incorrect because there must be a comma after *plausible*.

27. D: Choice *D* strengthens the overall sentence structure while condensing the words. This makes the subject of the sentence, and the emphasis of the writer, much clearer to the reader. Thus, while Choice *A* is technically correct, the language is choppy and over-complicated. Choice *B* is better but lacks the reference to a specific image of dinosaurs. Choice *C* introduces unnecessary commas.

28. B: Choice *B* correctly joins the two independent clauses. Choice *A* is decent, but "that would be" is too verbose for the sentence. Choice *C* incorrectly changes the semicolon to a comma. Choice *D* splits the clauses effectively but is not concise enough.

29. A: Choice *A* is correct, as the original sentence has no error. Choices *B* and *C* employ unnecessary semicolons and commas. Choice *D* would be an ideal revision, but it lacks the comma after *Ransom* that would enable the sentence structure to flow.

30. D: By reorganizing the sentence, the context becomes clearer with Choice *D*. Choice *A* has an awkward sentence structure. Choice *B* offers a revision that doesn't correspond well with the original sentence's intent. Choice *C* cuts out too much of the original content, losing the full meaning.

31. C: Choice *C* fixes the disagreement between the singular *this* and the plural *viewpoints*. Choice *A*, therefore, is incorrect. Choice *B* introduces an unnecessary comma. In Choice *D*, *those* agrees with *viewpoints*, but neither agrees with *distinguishes*.

32. A: Choice *A* is direct and clear, without any punctuation errors. Choice *B* is well-written but too wordy. Choice *C* adds an unnecessary comma. Choice *D* is also well-written but much less concise than Choice *A*.

33. D: Choice *D* rearranges the sentence to improve clarity and impact, with *tempting* directly describing *idea*. On its own, Choice *A* is a run-on. Choice *B* is better because it separates the clauses, but it keeps an unnecessary comma. Choice *C* is also an improvement but still a run-on.

34. B: Choice *B* is the best answer simply because the sentence makes it clear that Un-man takes over and possesses Weston. In Choice *A*, these events sounded like two different things, instead of an action and result. Choices *C* and *D* make this relationship clearer, but the revisions don't flow very well grammatically.

35. D: Changing the phrase *after this* to *then* makes the sentence less complicated and captures the writer's intent, making Choice *D* correct. Choice *A* is awkwardly constructed. Choices *B* and *C* misuse their commas and do not adequately improve the clarity.

36. B: By starting a new sentence, the run-on issue is eliminated, and a new line of reasoning can be seamlessly introduced, making Choice *B* correct. Choice *A* is thus incorrect. While Choice *C* fixes the run-on via a semicolon, a comma is still needed after *this*. Choice *D* contains a comma splice. The independent clauses must be separated by more than just a comma, even with the rearrangement of the second half of the sentence.

37. C: Choice *C* condenses the original sentence while being more active in communicating the emphasis on changing times/media that the author is going for, so it is correct. Choice *A* is clunky because it lacks a comma after *today* to successfully transition into the second half of the sentence. Choice *B* inserts unnecessary commas. Choice *D* is a good revision of the underlined section, but not only does it not fully capture the original meaning, it also does not flow into the rest of the sentence.

38. B: Choice *B* clearly illustrates the author's point, with a well-placed semicolon that breaks the sentence into clearer, more readable sections. Choice *A* lacks punctuation. Choice *C* is incorrect because the period inserted after *question* forms an incomplete sentence. Choice *D* is a very good revision but does not make the author's point clearer than the original.

39. A: Choice *A* is correct: while the sentence seems long, it actually doesn't require any commas. The conjunction "that" successfully combines the two parts of the sentence without the need for additional punctuation. Choices *B* and *C* insert commas unnecessarily, incorrectly breaking up the flow of the sentence. Choice *D* alters the meaning of the original text by creating a new sentence, which is only a fragment.

40. C: Choice *C* correctly replaces *for* with *to*, the correct preposition for the selected area. Choice *A* is not the answer because of this incorrect preposition. Choice *B* is unnecessarily long and disrupts the original sentence structure. Choice *D* is also too wordy and lacks parallel structure.

41. D: Choice *D* is the answer because it inserts the correct punctuation to fix the sentence, linking the dependent and independent clauses. Choice *A* is therefore incorrect. Choice *B* is also incorrect since this revision only adds content to the sentence while lacking grammatical precision. Choice *C* overdoes the punctuation; only a comma is needed, not a semicolon.

42. B: Choice *B* correctly separates the section into two sentences and changes the word order to make the second part clearer. Choice *A* is incorrect because it is a run-on. Choice *C* adds an extraneous comma, while Choice *D* makes the run-on worse and does not coincide with the overall structure of the sentence.

43. C: Choice *C* is the best answer because of how the commas are used to flank *in earnest*. This distinguishes the side thought (*in earnest*) from the rest of the sentence. Choice *A* needs punctuation. Choice *B* inserts a semicolon in a spot that doesn't make sense, resulting in a fragmented sentence and lost meaning. Choice *D* is unnecessarily repetitive and creates a run-on.

44. A: Choice *A* is correct because the sentence contains no errors. The comma after *bias* successfully links the two halves of the sentence, and the use of *it's* is correct as a contraction of *it is*. Choice *B* creates a sentence fragment, while Choice *C* creates a run-on. Choice *D* incorrectly changes *it's* to *its*.

45. D: Choice *D* correctly inserts a comma after *However* and fixes *over use* to *overuse*—in this usage, it is one word. Choice *A* is therefore incorrect, as is Choice *B*. Choice *C* is a good revision but does not fit well with the rest of the sentence.

Practice Test #2

Questions 1–9 are based on the following passage:

The name "Thor" has always been associated with great power. (1) <u>Arguably, Norse Mythologies most</u> popular and powerful god is Thor of the Aesir. My first experience of Thor was not like most of today's generation. I grew up reading Norse mythology where (2) <u>Thor wasn't a comic book superhero, but even mightier</u>. There are stories of Thor destroying mountains, (3) <u>defeating scores of giants and lifting up the world's largest creature the Midgard Serpent.</u> But always, Thor was a protector.

Like in modern comics and movies, Thor was the god of thunder and wielded (4) <u>the hammer Mjolnir however there are several differences</u> between the ancient legend and modern hero. (5) <u>For example, Loki, the god of mischief, isn't Thor's brother.</u> Loki is actually Thor's servant, but this doesn't stop the trickster from causing chaos, chaos that Thor has to then quell. In all of his incarnations, Thor is a god that reestablishes order by tempering the chaos around him. (6) <u>This is also symbolized in his prized weapon Mjolnir a magic hammer.</u> A hammer is both a weapon and a (7) <u>tool, but why would a god favor a seemingly everyday object?</u>

A hammer is used to shape metal and create change. The hammer tempers raw iron, (8) <u>ore that is in an chaotic state of impurities and shapelessness,</u> to create an item of worth. Thus, a hammer is in many ways a tool that brings a kind of order to the world—like Thor. Hammers were also tools of everyday people, which further endeared Thor to the common man. Therefore, it's no surprise that Thor remains an iconic hero to this day.

I began thinking to myself, why is Thor so prominent in our culture today even though many people don't follow the old religion? (9) <u>Well the truth is that every culture throughout time, including ours,</u> needs heroes. People need figures in their lives that give them hope and make them aspire to be great. We need the peace of mind that chaos will eventually be brought to order and that good can conquer evil. Thor was a figure of hope and remains so to this day.

1. Which of the following would be the best choice for this sentence (reproduced below)?

(1) <u>Arguably, Norse Mythologies most</u> popular and powerful god is Thor of the Aesir.

a. NO CHANGE
b. Arguably Norse Mythologies most
c. Arguably, Norse mythology's most
d. Arguably, Norse Mythology's most

2. Which of the following would be the best choice for this sentence (reproduced below)?

I grew up reading Norse mythology where (2) Thor wasn't a comic book superhero, but even mightier.

a. NO CHANGE
b. Thor wasn't a comic book superhero. He was even mightier.
c. Thor wasn't a comic book superhero but even mightier.
d. Thor wasn't a comic book superhero, he was even mightier.

3. Which of the following would be the best choice for this sentence (reproduced below)?

There are stories of Thor destroying mountains, (3) defeating scores of giants and lifting up the world's largest creature the Midgard Serpent.

a. NO CHANGE
b. defeating scores of giants, and lifting up the world's largest creature, the Midgard Serpent.
c. defeating scores of giants, and lifting up the world's largest creature the Midgard Serpent.
d. defeating scores, of giants, and lifting up the world's largest creature the Midgard Serpent.

4. Which of the following would be the best choice for this sentence (reproduced below)?

Like in modern comics and movies, Thor was the god of thunder and wielded (4) the hammer Mjolnir however there are several differences between the ancient legend and modern hero.

a. NO CHANGE
b. the hammer Mjolnir, however there are several differences
c. the hammer Mjolnir. However there are several differences
d. the hammer Mjolnir. However, there are several differences

5. Which of the following would be the best choice for this sentence (reproduced below)?

(5) For example, Loki, the god of mischief, isn't Thor's brother.

a. NO CHANGE
b. For example, Loki the god of mischief isn't Thor's brother.
c. For example, Loki the god of mischief, isn't Thor's brother.
d. For example Loki, the god of mischief, isn't Thor's brother.

6. Which of the following would be the best choice for this sentence (reproduced below)?

(6) This is also symbolized in his prized weapon Mjolnir a magic hammer.

a. NO CHANGE
b. This is also symbolized in his prized weapon, Mjolnir a magic hammer.
c. This is also symbolized in his prized weapon, Mjolnir, a magic hammer.
d. This is also symbolized in his prized weapon Mjolnir, a magic hammer.

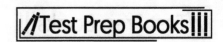

7. Which of the following would be the best choice for this sentence (reproduced below)?

A hammer is both a weapon and a (7) <u>tool, but why would a god favor a seemingly everyday object?</u>

a. NO CHANGE
b. tool; why would a god favor a seemingly everyday object?
c. tool, but, why would a god favor a seemingly everyday object?
d. tool, however, why would a god favor a seemingly everyday object?

8. Which of the following would be the best choice for this sentence (reproduced below)?

The hammer tempers raw iron, (8) <u>ore that is in an chaotic state of impurities and shapelessness,</u> to create an item of worth.

a. NO CHANGE
b. ore that is in a chaotic state of impurities and shapelessness
c. ore that has the impurities and shapelessness of a chaotic state
d. ore that is in an chaotic state, of impurities and shapelessness,

9. Which of the following would be the best choice for this sentence (reproduced below)?

(9) <u>Well the truth is that every culture throughout time, including ours,</u> needs heroes.

a. NO CHANGE
b. Well, the truth is, every culture throughout time, including ours,
c. Well, every culture throughout time, including ours, in truth
d. Well, the truth is that every culture throughout time, including ours,

Questions 10–18 are based on the following passage:

In our essay and class discussion, (10) <u>we came to talking about</u> mirrors. It was an excellent class in which we focused on an article written by Salman Rushdie that compared the homeland to a mirror. (11) <u>Essentially this mirror was an metaphor for us and our homeland.</u> (12) <u>When we look at our reflection we see the culture, our homeland staring back at us.</u> An interesting analogy, but the conversation really began when we read that Rushdie himself stated that the cracked mirror is more valuable than a whole one. But why?

(13) <u>After reflecting on the passage I found the answer to be simple.</u> The analogy reflects the inherent nature of human individuality. The cracks in the mirror represent different aspects of our own being. Perhaps it is our personal views, our hobbies, or our differences with other people, but (14) <u>whatever it is that makes us unique defines us, even while we are part of a big culture.</u> (15) <u>What this tells us is that we can have a homeland, but ultimately we ourselves are each different in it.</u>

Just because one's (16) <u>mirror is cracked, the individuals isn't disowned</u> from the actual, physical homeland and culture within. It means that the homeland is uniquely perceived by the (17) <u>individual beholding it and that there are in fact many aspects </u>to culture itself. Like the various cracks, a culture has religion, language, and many other factors that form to make it whole. What this idea does is invite the viewer to accept their own view of their culture as a whole.

Like in Chandra's *Love and Longing in Bombay*, a single homeland has many stories to tell. Whether one is a cop or a retired war veteran, the individual will perceive the different aspects of the world with unduplicated eyes. (18) Rushdie, seems to be urging those his readers to love their culture but to not be pressured by the common crowd. Again, the cracks represent differences which could easily be interpreted as views about the culture, so what this is saying is to accept the culture but accept oneself as well.

From the essay "Portals to Homeland: Mirrors"

10. Which of the following would be the best choice for this sentence (reproduced below)?

In our essay and class discussion, (10) we came to talking about mirrors.

a. NO CHANGE
b. we were talking about
c. we talked about
d. we came to talk about

11. Which of the following would be the best choice for this sentence (reproduced below)?

(11) Essentially this mirror is an metaphor for us and our homeland.

a. NO CHANGE
b. Essentially, this mirror is a metaphor for us and our homeland.
c. Essentially, this mirror is an metaphor for us and our homeland.
d. Essentially this mirror is an metaphor, for us and our homeland.

12. Which of the following would be the best choice for this sentence (reproduced below)?

(12) When we look at our reflection we see the culture, our homeland staring back at us.

a. NO CHANGE
b. When we look at our reflection we see our culture our homeland staring back at us.
c. When we look at our reflection we saw our culture, our homeland, staring back at us.
d. Looking at our reflection we see our culture as our homeland is staring back at us.

13. Which of the following would be the best choice for this sentence (reproduced below)?

(13) After reflecting on the passage I found the answer to be simple.

a. NO CHANGE
b. After reflecting on the passage; I found the answer to be simple.
c. After reflecting on the passage I finding the answer to be simple.
d. After reflecting on the passage, I found the answer to be simple.

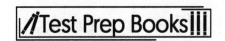

14. Which of the following would be the best choice for this sentence (reproduced below)?

Perhaps it is our personal views, our hobbies, or our differences with other people, but (14) <u>whatever it is that makes us unique defines us, even while we are part of a big culture.</u>

a. NO CHANGE
b. whatever it is, that makes us unique, defines us, even while we are part of a big culture.
c. whatever it is that makes us unique also defines us, even while we are part of a bigger culture.
d. whatever it is that makes us unique defines us, even though we are part of a big culture.

15. Which of the following would be the best choice for this sentence (reproduced below)?

(15) <u>What this tells us is that we can have a homeland, but ultimately we ourselves are each different in it.</u>

a. NO CHANGE
b. What this tells us is that we can have a homeland, but ultimately, we ourselves are each different in it.
c. What this tells us is that we can have a homeland, however, ultimately, we ourselves are each different in it.
d. What this tells us is that we can have a homeland, ultimately we ourselves are each different in it.

16. Which of the following would be the best choice for this sentence (reproduced below)?

Just because one's (16) <u>mirror is cracked, the individuals isn't disowned</u> from the actual, physical homeland and culture within.

a. NO CHANGE
b. mirror is cracked, the individuals will not be disowned
c. mirror is cracked, the individuals aren't disowned
d. mirror is cracked, the individual isn't disowned

17. Which of the following would be the best choice for this sentence (reproduced below)?

It means that the homeland is uniquely perceived by the (17) <u>individual beholding it and that there are, in fact, many aspects</u> of culture itself.

a. NO CHANGE
b. individual beholding it; and that there are in fact many aspects
c. individual beholding it and that there is, in fact, many aspects
d. individual beholding it and there's in fact, many aspects

18. Which of the following would be the best choice for this sentence (reproduced below)?

(18) <u>Rushdie, seems to be urging those his readers</u> to love their culture but to not be pressured by the common crowd.

a. NO CHANGE
b. Rushdie seemed to be urging his readers
c. Rushdie, seeming to urge his readers,
d. Rushdie seems to be urging his readers

Questions 19–27 are based on the following passage:

The Odyssey reading performed by Odds Bodkin (19) <u>was an especially rewarding experience</u>. Myths continue to help us (20) <u>understood ancient cultures</u> while still helping us connect to real-world lessons through narrative. (21) <u>While myths were not read exactly the way Bodkin performed *The Odyssey*,</u> his performance truly combined ancient and modern artistic styles.

(22) <u>Originally, myths were not written down instead, stories like The Odyssey</u> were transferred to written form thousands of years after they were originally told. *Told* is a (23) <u>key term here: myths were passing on to generations orally</u>. They were sung, or at least accompanied by music. Of course, we no longer gather in halls to hear (24) <u>myths; we read it, or</u> perhaps listen to audio versions. The Odds Bodkin reading was unique in that it offered a traditional glimpse into what it might have been like to receive a myth in its original form of delivery.

What I thought was especially interesting, was that Bodkin used his guitar to build an atmosphere or tempo around the story. In points of action, like when the wooden horse was being moved into Troy, or when Odysseus leads his men in search of the missing crew (lotus episode), he played a signature tune. (25) <u>This creates a kind of soundtrack for the story,</u> providing a unique feeling for the scene. While (26) <u>there is no visual stimuli like in motion picture</u>, one is moved by the guitar's playing. Accompanied by his dramatic reading, the music reflects the action of the plot and even emotions/insights of the characters. Interestingly, Bodkin also used physical gestures to tell the story as well. He occasionally acted out scenes with his hands and sometimes with sound effects.

The best scene was when Bodkin played the Cyclops, Polyphemus, grabbing and gorging himself on Odysseus' men. (27) <u>In addition from bringing a kind of animation</u> to the presentation, it linked the story to the physical world too. He wasn't just reading, he was acting. It gave this a three-dimensional aspect of the telling of *The Odyssey* that I thought was especially great.

19. Which of the following would be the best choice for this sentence (reproduced below)?

The Odyssey reading performed by Odds Bodkin (19) <u>was an especially rewarding experience.</u>

a. NO CHANGE
b. was, an especially, rewarding experience.
c. was a especially rewarding experience.
d. was an especially rewarded experience.

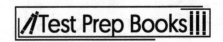

20. Which of the following would be the best choice for this sentence (reproduced below)?

Myths continue to help us (20) <u>understood ancient cultures</u> while still helping us connect to real-world lessons through narrative.

a. NO CHANGE
b. understand ancient cultures
c. understood ancient cultures,
d. understanding ancient cultures

21. Which of the following would be the best choice for this sentence (reproduced below)?

(21) <u>While myths were not read exactly the way Bodkin performed The Odyssey,</u> his performance truly combined ancient and modern artistic styles.

a. NO CHANGE
b. While myths were not exactly the way Bodkin read/performed *The Odyssey*,
c. While myths were not read, exactly, the way Bodkin performed *The Odyssey*,
d. While myths were not read exactly the way Bodkin performed *The Odyssey*.

22. Which of the following would be the best choice for this sentence (reproduced below)?

(22) <u>Originally, myths were not written down instead, stories like The Odyssey</u> were transferred to written form thousands of years after they were originally told.

a. NO CHANGE
b. Myths, originally, were not written down instead, stories like *The Odyssey*
c. Originally myths were not written down; instead stories like *The Odyssey*
d. Originally, myths were not written down. Instead, stories like *The Odyssey*

23. Which of the following would be the best choice for this sentence (reproduced below)?

Told is a (23) <u>key term here: myths were passing on to generations orally.</u>

a. NO CHANGE
b. key term here: myths were passed on to generations orally.
c. key term here: myths passed on to generations orally.
d. key term here: myths pass on to generations orally.

24. Which of the following would be the best choice for this sentence (reproduced below)?

Of course, we no longer gather in halls to hear (24) <u>myths, we read it, or</u> perhaps listen to audio versions.

a. NO CHANGE
b. myths; we read it or
c. myths; they are read, or
d. myths; we read them, or

25. Which of the following would be the best choice for this sentence (reproduced below)?

(25) <u>This creates a kind of soundtrack for the story,</u> providing a unique feeling for the scene.

a. NO CHANGE
b. This creates a kind of soundtrack for the story;
c. This creates, a kind of soundtrack, for the story,
d. This creates a kinds of soundtrack for the story,

26. Which of the following would be the best choice for this sentence (reproduced below)?

While (26) <u>there is no visual stimuli like in motion picture,</u> one is moved by the guitar's playing.

a. NO CHANGE
b. there is no visual stimuli, like in motion picture,
c. there are no visual stimuli, like in motion pictures,
d. there are no visual stimuli like in motion picture,

27. Which of the following would be the best choice for this sentence (reproduced below)?

(27) <u>In addition from bringing a kind of animation</u> to the presentation, it linked the story to the physical world too.

a. NO CHANGE
b. In addition to bringing a kind of animation
c. In addition too bringing, a kind of animation,
d. In addition for bringing a kind of animation

Questions 28–36 are based on the following passage:

Quantum mechanics, which describes how the universe works on its smallest scale, is inherently weird. Even the founders of the field (28) <u>including Max Planck, Werner Heisenberg, and Wolfgang Pauli unsettled by the new theories' implications.</u> (29) <u>Instead of a deterministic world where everything can be predicted by equations,</u> events at the quantum scale are purely probabilistic. (30) <u>Every outcome exist simultaneously,</u> while the actual act of observation forces nature to choose one path.

In our everyday lives, (31) <u>this concept of determinism, is actually expressed</u> in the thought experiment of Schrödinger's cat. Devised by Erwin Schrödinger, one of the founders of quantum mechanics, (32) <u>it's purpose is to show how truly strange</u> the framework is. Picture a box containing a cat, a radioactive element, and a vial of poison. (33) <u>If the radioactive element decays, it will release the poison and kill the cat.</u> The box is closed, so there is no way for anyone outside to know what is happening inside. Since the cat's status—alive and dead—are mutually exclusive, only one state can exist. (34) <u>What quantum mechanics says however</u> is that the cat is simultaneously alive and dead, existing in both states until the box's lid is removed and one outcome is chosen.

(35) <u>Further confounding our sense of reality, Louis de Broglie proposed that, on the smallest scales, particles and waves are indistinguishable.</u> This builds on Albert Einstein's famous theory that matter and energy are interchangeable. Although there isn't apparent evidence for this in

our daily lives, various experiments have shown the validity of quantum mechanics. One of the most famous experiments is the double-slit experiment, which initially proved the wave nature of light. When shone through parallel slits onto a screen, (36) light creates a interference pattern of alternating bands of light and dark. But when electrons were fired at the slits, the act of observation changed the outcome. If observers monitored which slit the electrons travelled through, only one band was seen on the screen. This is expected, since we know electrons act as particles. However, when they monitored the screen only, an interference pattern is created—implying that the electrons behaved as waves!

28. Which of the following would be the best choice for this sentence (reproduced below)?

(28) Even the founders of the field including Max Planck, Werner Heisenberg, and Wolfgang Pauli unsettled by the new theories' implications.

a. NO CHANGE
b. including Max Planck, Werner Heisenberg, and Wolfgang Pauli; unsettled by the new theories' implications.
c. including Max Planck, Werner Heisenberg, and Wolfgang Pauli were unsettled by the new theories' implications.
d. including Max Planck, Werner Heisenberg, and Wolfgang Pauli were unsettled by the new theory's implications.

29. Which of the following would be the best choice for this sentence (reproduced below)?

(29) Instead of a deterministic world where everything can be predicted by equations, events at the quantum scale are purely probabilistic.

a. NO CHANGE
b. Instead, of a deterministic world where everything can be predicted by equations,
c. Instead of a deterministic world where everything can be predicting by equations,
d. Instead of a deterministic world, where everything can be predicted by equations,

30. Which of the following would be the best choice for this sentence (reproduced below)?

(30) Every outcome exist simultaneously, while the actual act of observation forces nature to choose one path.

a. NO CHANGE
b. Each of these outcome exist simultaneously,
c. Every outcome, existing simultaneously,
d. Every outcome exists simultaneously,

31. Which of the following would be the best choice for this sentence (reproduced below)?

   In our everyday lives, (31) this concept of determinism, is actually expressed in the thought
   experiment of Schrödinger's cat.

   a. NO CHANGE
   b. this concept of determinism is actually expressed
   c. this, concept of determinism, is actually expressed
   d. this concept of determinism, is expressed actually

32. Which of the following would be the best choice for this sentence (reproduced below)?

   Devised by Erwin Schrödinger, one of the founders of quantum mechanics, (32) it's purpose is to
   show how truly strange the framework is.

   a. NO CHANGE
   B. its purposes is to show how truly strange
   c. its purpose is to show how truly strange
   d. it's purpose, showing how truly strange

33. Which of the following would be the best choice for this sentence (reproduced below)?

   (33) If the radioactive element decays, it will release the poison and kill the cat.

   a. NO CHANGE
   b. If, the radioactive element decays, it will release the poison and kill the cat.
   c. If the radioactive element decays. It will release the poison and kill the cat.
   d. If the radioactive element decays, releasing the poison and kill the cat.

34. Which of the following would be the best choice for this sentence (reproduced below)?

   (34) What quantum mechanics says however is that the cat is simultaneously alive and dead,
   existing in both states until the box's lid is removed and one outcome is chosen.

   a. NO CHANGE
   b. What quantum mechanics says however, is
   c. What quantum mechanics says. However, is
   d. What quantum mechanics says, however, is

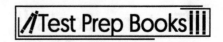

35. Which of the following would be the best choice for this sentence (reproduced below)?

(35) Further confounding our sense of reality, Louis de Broglie proposed that, on the smallest scales, particles and waves are indistinguishable.

a. NO CHANGE
b. Further confounding our sense of reality Louis de Broglie proposed that on the smallest scales, particles and waves are indistinguishable.
c. Further confounding our sense of reality, Louis de Broglie proposed that on the smallest scales, particles and waves are indistinguishable.
d. Further, confounding our sense of reality, Louis de Broglie proposed that, on the smallest scales, particles and waves are indistinguishable.

36. Which of the following would be the best choice for this sentence (reproduced below)?

When shone through parallel slits onto a screen, (36) light creates a interference pattern of alternating bands of light and dark.

a. NO CHANGE
b. light created an interference
c. lights create a interference
d. light, creating an interference,

Questions 37–45 are based on the following passage:

(37) As the adage goes knowledge is power. Those who are smart and understand the world as it is are the most fit to lead. Intelligence (38) doesn't necessarily require a deep understanding of complex scientific principles. Rather, having the basic knowledge of how the world works, particularly how people go about gaining what they need to survive and thrive, (39) are more important.

Any leadership position, whether on the job or informally, tends to be fraught with politics. (40) Smart leaders will engage in critical thinking allowing them to discern ulterior motives and identify propaganda. Besides catching negative intentions, (41) these practice will serve to highlight the positives in group interactions. Gaining insights into different viewpoints will make leaders more (42) receptive to constructive criticism and ideas from unexpected sources. As with many aspects of being a good and well-rounded person, the seeds for this trait are sown in pre-school. Besides facts and figures, students need to be taught critical thinking skills to survive in a world flooded with subliminal messages and scams. (43) Sadly our current society is plagued by many inconvenient truths that are attacked as lies. Wise leaders should recognize when someone is trying to save the world or merely push a political agenda.

Just as important as the knowledge of how the world works (44) is understood of how humanity operates. Leaders should be able to tactfully make friends and influence people using the doctrines of psychology. People who say whatever comes into their heads without thinking demonstrate a lack of basic diplomatic understanding, not to mention a deficiency of self-control and lack of respect. Breaches of courtesy, whether intentional or otherwise, strain relations and can ruin potential alliances.

While the best leaders are tolerant of other (45) <u>cultural practices and diverse perspectives, those who exhibit disregard</u> and unwarranted contempt for others shouldn't be expected to find favor. Knowledge extends past textbook learning to practical awareness, encompassing skills for a successful life as a decent human being all around. These skills include risk management and creative solutions. Someone who fails to hone these abilities—or neglects to apply their knowledge—will likely be overthrown by those they are supposed to lead.

37. Which of the following would be the best choice for this sentence (reproduced below)?

(37) <u>As the adage goes knowledge is power.</u>

a. NO CHANGE
b. Knowledge is power as the adage goes.
c. As the adage goes, "knowledge is power."
d. As, the adage goes, knowledge is power.

38. Which of the following would be the best choice for this sentence (reproduced below)?

Intelligence (38) <u>doesn't necessarily require</u> a deep understanding of complex scientific principles.

a. NO CHANGE
b. doesn't, necessarily, require
c. doesn't require necessarily
d. aren't necessarily require

39. Which of the following would be the best choice for this sentence (reproduced below)?

Rather, having the basic knowledge of how the world works, particularly how people go about gaining what they need to survive and thrive, (39) <u>are more important.</u>

a. NO CHANGE
b. is more important.
c. are the most important.
d. is most important.

40. Which of the following would be the best choice for this sentence (reproduced below)?

(40) <u>Smart leaders will engage in critical thinking allowing them to discern ulterior motives and identify propaganda.</u>

a. NO CHANGE
b. Smart leaders will engage in critical thinking allowing them to discern ulterior motives, and identify propaganda.
c. Smart leaders will engage in critical thinking, allowing them to discern ulterior motives and identify propaganda.
d. Smart leaders will engage in critical thinking allows them to discern ulterior motives and identify propaganda.

41. Which of the following would be the best choice for this sentence (reproduced below)?

Besides catching negative intentions, (41) <u>these practice will serve to highlight</u> the positives in group interactions.

a. NO CHANGE
b. this practices will serve to highlight
c. these practice serve to highlight
d. this practice will serve to highlight

42. Which of the following would be the best choice for this sentence (reproduced below)?

Gaining insights into different viewpoints will make leaders more (42) <u>receptive to constructive criticism and ideas from unexpected sources.</u>

a. NO CHANGE
b. receptive for constructive criticism and ideas from unexpected sources.
c. receptive from unexpected sources to construct criticism and ideas.
d. receptive, to constructive criticism and ideas, from unexpected sources.

43. Which of the following would be the best choice for this sentence (reproduced below)?

(43) <u>Sadly our current society is plagued by many inconvenient truths that are attacked as lies.</u>

a. NO CHANGE
b. Sadly, our current society is plagued by many inconvenient truths that are attacked as lies.
c. Sadly our current society is plagued by many inconvenient truths, that are attacked as lies.
d. Sadly our current society is plaguing by many inconvenient truths that are attacking as lies.

44. Which of the following would be the best choice for this sentence (reproduced below)?

Just as important as the knowledge of how the world works (44) <u>is understood of how humanity operates.</u>

a. NO CHANGE
b. is to understand of how humanity operates.
c. is understanding of how humanity operates.
d. is an understanding of how humanity operates.

Answer Explanations #2

1. C: Choice *C* is correct, changing *Mythologies* to *mythology's*. Since one myth system is being referred to—and one particular component of it—the possessive is needed. Additionally, *Mythology's* does not need to be capitalized, since only the culture represents a proper noun. Choice *A* therefore is incorrect, with Choice *B* failing to fix the plural and Choice *D* having extraneous capitalization.

2. A: Choice *A* is correct because the sentence has no issues. While Choice *B* separates the sentence correctly, it makes more sense in this context of a direct comparison to keep the sentence intact. Choice *C* is incorrect because the sentence needs a comma after *superhero*. Choice *D* is unnecessarily long and lacks the word *but* that helps the author differentiate ideas.

3. B: Choice *B* is correct because it adds the two commas needed to clarify key subjects individually and establish a better flow to the sentence. Since *destroying mountains*, *defeating scores of giants*, and *lifting up the world's largest creature* are separate feats, commas are needed to separate them. Also, because *the world's largest creature* can stand alone in the sentence, a comma needs to proceed its name; *the Midgard Serpent* is not necessary to the sentence but rather provides extra information as an aside. Choice *A* is unclear and thus incorrect. Choice *C* is still missing a comma, while Choice *D* put an extraneous one in an incorrect place.

4. D: Choice *D* is correct since the sentence is lengthy as originally presented and should be split into two. Additionally, the word *however*, being a conjunction, needs a comma afterwards. Choice *A* is therefore incorrect due to missing punctuation. Choice *B* is an improvement but could separate the sentence's ideas better and more clearly. Choice *C* lacks the necessary comma after the word *however*.

5. A: Choice *A* is correct because this sentence has no issues with punctuation, content, or sentence construction. While there are three commas used, they serve to appropriately introduce an idea, an individual person, and transition into another line of thinking. Choices *B* and *C* miss commas needed to offset Loki's title as *the god of mischief*, while Choice *D* misses the comma needed to introduce the example.

6. C: Choice *C* is correct because the sentence needs two commas to emphasize the proper name of Mjolnir. Since Mjolnir is being talked about, directly addressed, and then explained, it must be flanked by commas to signify its role in the sentence. Choice *A* lacks necessary punctuation and is confusing. Choices *B* and *D* miss commas on either side of *Mjolnir*.

7. A: Choice *A* is correct, as this is an example of a compound sentence written correctly. Because of the conjunction *but* and the proceeding comma, the two independent clauses are able to form a single sentence coherently. While Choice *B* makes the question more direct, it doesn't go well with the remainder of the sentence. Choice *C* applies a comma after *but*, which is incorrect and confusing. Choice *D* inserts *however*, which is out of place and makes the sentence awkward.

8. B: Choice *B* correctly changes *an* to *a*, since *an* is only required when *a* precedes a word that begins with a vowel. Choice *A* therefore uses the incorrect form of *a*. Choice *C* fixes the issue but unnecessarily reverses the structure of the sentence, making it less direct and more confusing. Choice *D* does not fix the error and adds extraneous commas.

9. D: Choice *D* is correct, simply applying a comma after *Well* to introduce an idea. Choice *A* is therefore incorrect. Choice *B* introduces too many commas, resulting in a fractured sentence structure. Choice *C*

applies a comma after *Well*, which is correct, but interrupts the flow of the sentence by switching the structure of the sentence. This makes the sentence lack fluidity and serves to confuse the reader.

10. C: Choice *C* is simple and straightforward, describing the event clearly for the reader to follow; talked is past tense, which is consistent with the rest of the passage. Choice *A* is incorrect, since we came to talking about confuses the tense of the sentence and the verb talk. Choices *B* and *D* are wordy and not as straightforward as Choice *C*.

11. B: Choice *B* is the correct answer because it adds a comma after *Essentially* and changes *an* to *a*. This is called the indefinite article, when an unspecified thing or quantity is referred to. However, *an* doesn't agree with *metaphor*, since *an* should only be used when the next word starts with a vowel. Choice *A* uses the article *an* and lacks the crucial comma after *Essentially*. Choice *C* is incorrect because it only provides the comma after *Essentially*, neglecting the indefinite article disagreement. Choice *D* is incorrect because neither issue is fixed and an unnecessary comma is introduced.

12. A: Choice *A* is correct because there are no errors present in the sentence. Choice *B* is a run on, because the clauses are not broken up by commas. Choice *C* has a verbal disagreement: *look* and *saw* are different tenses. Choice *D* changes the structure of the sentence but fails to add a transition to make this correct.

13. D: Choice *D* is correct because it uses a comma after the word *passage*, successfully connecting the dependent clause with its independent clause to form a complete thought/sentence. Choice *A* is therefore incorrect. Choice *B* uses a semicolon unwisely. The two clauses need to be connected to each other in order to make sense, otherwise they are just two fragments improperly combined. Choice *C* does not have the required comma and changes *found* to *finding*, an inappropriate tense for the verb in this sentence.

14. C: Choice *C* is correct because it fixes two major flaws in the original portion of the sentence. First, it inserts the adverb *also* to show the connection between *whatever it is that makes us unique* and *defines us*. Without this adverb, the sentence lacks clarity, and the connection is lost. Second, *big* is incorrect in this context. The sentence needs the superlative *bigger* in order to communicate the scope and scale of the author's assessment of how people relate to others on a grand scale. Choice *A* is therefore incorrect, Choice *B* inserts unnecessary commas, and Choice *D* subtly alters the original meaning.

15. B: Choice *B* is correct because a comma is correctly inserted after *ultimately*. This serves to express a side thought that helps transition into the rest of the sentence without having to break it apart. Choice *A* is incorrect because it lacks the comma after *ultimately*. Choice *C* uses too many commas and is overly complicated. Choice *D* lacks the necessary conjunction after the comma (*but*) before *ultimately*, making it a run-on sentence. It also lacks the important comma after *ultimately*.

16. D: Choice *D* corrects the subject-verb disagreement. *One's* is the possessive form of *one*, a single individual, not the plural *individuals*. *Isn't* is the singular contraction of *is not*, which conflicts with *individuals*. To correct this, either *isn't* must change to *aren't* or *individuals* should become the singular *individual*. The latter is correct because of the context of the sentence. Choice *A* is incorrect because of the subject-verb disagreement. Choice *B* uses the future tense, while Choice *C's aren't* conflicts with *one's*, which is possessive singular.

17. A: Choice *A* contains no grammatical errors and communicates the writer's message clearly. Choice *B* inserts an unnecessary semicolon. Choice *C* uses *is*, which disagrees with the plural *aspects*. *Are* must be used because it is plural. This is the same for Choice *D*, which uses *there's* (*there is*).

18. D: Choice *D* is the correct answer because it removes the comma after *Rushdie*. Adding a comma after the proper name in this case is incorrect because *Rushdie* is not being addressed directly. Rather, the writer is talking about Rushdie. Therefore, Choices *A* disrupts the construction of the sentence. Choice *B* is incorrect because *seemed*, in this context, should be present tense. The author is talking about a theme and idea that *Rushdie* had but that is still relevant and being actively studied. Choice *C* fails to remove the comma after Rushdie and applies the gerund *seeming* incorrectly.

19. A: Choice *A* is the correct answer. The sentence requires no punctuation and clearly communicates the author's idea. Choice *B* is incorrect because it misuses multiple commas. Choice *C* is incorrect because it uses *a* instead of *an*, which is necessary because the next word (*essentially*) begins with a vowel. Choice *D* changes *rewarding* to *rewarded*, which clashes with the earlier use of *was*, indicating past tense, making it incorrect.

20. B: Choice *B* is correct because it uses the present tense of *understand* instead of the past tense *understood*. *Continues* emphasizes something ongoing. Therefore, the present tense of *understand* is needed. Choice *A* therefore has tense disagreement. Choice *C* uses an extraneous comma. While Choice *D's* use of the gerund is a better option, *in* would need to be added before *understanding* for correctness.

21. A: Choice *A* is correct; the dependent and independent clauses are successfully combined to form a sentence. Choice *A* is also the most concise and straightforward option, presenting the information appropriately so as not to be confusing. Choice *B* can be eliminated because it changes the meaning of the sentence. Choice *C* unnecessarily flanks *exactly* with commas. Choice *D* is incorrect because a period after the underlined phrase would result in an incomplete sentence.

22. D: Choice *D* is correct because of how it successfully connects the two sentences. By starting a new sentence with *instead*, the two ideas are clearly and correctly presented. Choice *A* is a run-on. Choice *B* is incorrect because the commas used are misplaced and confusing. Choice *C* is incorrect because there needs to be a comma after *originally*.

23. B: Choice *B* correctly uses the word *passed* instead of *passing*. The word *were* is being used as a past tense modifier; therefore, it disagrees with the *passing* participle. Combining the helping verb *were* with the past tense *passed* creates the correct past tense compound verb, *were passed*, which is needed to be grammatically consistent with the rest of the sentence. Choices *A*, *C*, and *D* thus have incongruent tenses.

24. D: Choice *D* is correct because it corrects the subject-verb disagreement between the plural *myths* and the singular *it*. This is done by changing *it* to *them*, reflecting that more than one type of *myths* are being talked about. Because of the subject-verb disagreement, Choice *A* is incorrect. Choice *B* does not correct this at all. Choice *C* addresses this disagreement, but at the cost of maintaining parallel structure within the sentence.

25. A: Choice *A* is correct because this sentence contains no grammatical errors, unlike the others. Choice *B* uses the semicolon when only a comma is required. Choice *C* uses commas to unnecessarily isolate *a kind of soundtrack* from its connected phrase. Choice *D* is incorrect because the plural *kinds* disagrees with the singular pronoun *This*.

26. C: Choice *C* is the correct answer because the plural *are* and *motion pictures* agree with the subject *stimuli* (the plural form of *stimulus*). All verbs and nouns in the sentence should be in agreement with each other in tense and number. Choices *A*, *B*, and *D* all violate this number agreement.

27. B: Choice *B* correctly replaces the preposition *from* with the correct proposition *to*. *To* is used to emphasize an action or idea being presented rather than received. This is why Choice *A* is incorrect. Choice *C* is incorrect because it uses the adverb *too*, which emphasizes a higher level of something or the addition of something in a sentence; this isn't relevant here. Choice *D* uses the preposition *for* instead of *to*.

28. C: Choice *C* is correct because it adds the helping verb *were* to modify *unsettled*. This allows the sentence to reflect that the founders were unsettled by the implications. Without *were* to connect *the founders* to *unsettled*, the sentence doesn't make sense. Choice *A* lacks the crucial helping verb, making it incorrect. Choice *B* is incorrect because of its unnecessary semicolon. Choice *D* changes *theories'*, which is plural possessive, to *theory's* (singular possessive), which isn't consistent with the sentence's context.

29. A: Choice *A* is correct because it contains no errors and requires no additional punctuation to form a coherent sentence. The single comma, used successfully, unites the two clauses and enables a solid grammatical structure. Choice *B* incorrectly places a comma after *Instead*, Choice *C* incorrectly changes *predicted* to *predicting*, and Choice *D* incorrectly separates *where everything can be predicted by equations* from the rest of the sentence.

30. D: Choice *D* is correct because it fixes the subject-verb disagreement with *Every outcome* and *exist*. *Exists* is third person present but also appropriate to reflect multiple outcomes, as indicated by *every outcome*. Choices *A* and *B* use *exist*, not *exists*, which makes them both incorrect. Choice *C* is fine on its own but does not fit with the rest of the sentence.

31. B: Choice *B* is correct because the comma after *determinism* isn't needed. Adding a comma in the selected area actually breaks up the independent clause of the sentence, thus compromising the overall structure of the sentence. Choices *A*, *C*, and *D* are therefore incorrect.

32. C: Choice *C* is the correct answer because it removes the contraction of *it is*, *it's*. Choice *A*, which is incorrect, originally used *it's*—note the apostrophe before *s*. *It's* simply means *it is*, while *its* (no apostrophe) shows possession. In this sentence, *its* is referring to the idea devised by Schrödinger, giving ownership of the purpose to the idea. Choice *B* is incorrect because *purpose* should remain singular. Choice *D* is incorrect because it uses *it's*.

33. A: Choice *A* is correct because the sentence is well-formed and grammatically correct. Choice *B* is incorrect because it adds an unnecessary comma after *if*. Choice *C* breaks the sentence apart, creating a sentence fragment. Choice *D* is incorrect because it changes *release* to a gerund and fails to make a coherent sentence, leaving only two dependent clauses.

34. D: Choice *D* is the correct answer. This is a tricky question, but Choice *D* is correct because, in the context of this sentence, it's important to have *however* flanked by commas. This is because the use of *however* is basically an aside to the reader, addressing an idea and then redirecting the reader to an alternative outcome or line of reasoning. Choice *A* is therefore confusing, with *however* floating in the sentence aimlessly. Choice *B* only uses one comma, which is incorrect. Choice *C* creates two incomplete sentences.

35. A: Choice *A* is correct. The sentence uses a lot of commas, but these are used effectively to highlight key points while continuing to focus on a central idea. Choice *B* is incorrect because the commas after *reality* and *that* are required. Choice *C* is incorrect because there should be a comma after *that* because *on the smallest scales* elaborates on the idea itself but not necessarily what Broglie said. Choice *D* puts a comma after *further*, which is unnecessary in this context.

36. B: Choice *B* correctly uses *an* instead of *a* to modify *interference*. The indefinite article *an* must be used before words that start with a vowel sound. The verb *created* is also in agreement with the tense of the story. Choice *C* incorrectly changes *creates* to *create* and pluralizes *light*, which is inconsistent with the rest of the sentence. Choice *D* modifies *creates* inappropriately and adds an incorrect comma after *light*.

37. C: Choice *C* is correct because it applies the single comma needed to combine the independent clause with the dependent clause, forming a functional sentence. It also includes quotes. Choice *A* is an awkward, disjointed sentence because it lacks a comma after *goes*. The other answers result in oddly constructed sentences (Choice *B*), and a misused comma after *As* (Choice *D*).

38. A: Choice *A* is the correct answer because the proper contraction for does not (doesn't) is used. There is also no need for commas or punctuation here as well, making Choices *B* and *C* incorrect. Choice *D* needlessly changes *doesn't* to *aren't*.

39. B: Choice *B* is correct because it fixes the subject-verb disagreement between the subject *the basic knowledge* and the verb *are*. Because *knowledge* is singular, the verb *are*, which is plural, is incorrect. Instead, the singular *is* must be used in place of *are*. This makes Choices *A* and *C* incorrect. Choice *D* is incorrect because it changes the meaning of the sentence.

40. C: Choice *C* is the correct answer because it employs a comma to effectively combine the independent clause with the dependent clause to form a complete sentence. Choice *A* lacks the comma after *thinking* needed to unite the two parts of the sentence. The independent clause is *Smart leaders will engage in critical thinking*, while the independent clause is *allowing them to discern ulterior motives and identify propaganda*. Choice *B* incorrectly adds a comma after *motives*. Choice *D* is incorrect because it still lacks connective punctuation and incorrectly alters the gerund *allowing* to *allows*; this would be fine if a comma and *which* were added before *allows* to effectively combine the clauses.

41. D: Choice *D* is the best answer because it changes *these* to *this*, making it properly modify the singular *practice*. Choice *A* is incorrect because of this lack of numerical agreement. Choice *B* is incorrect for the same reason—*this* is singular while *practices* is plural. Choice *C* is also incorrect because it doesn't fix *these* and takes out *will*, which is important for the tense of the overall sentence.

42. A: Choice *A* is correct because the sentence is fine as it is. Commas are not necessary here. Choices *B* and *C* replace *to* with *for* and *from*, respectively, which don't work in the context of the sentence: if leaders are *receptive*, they are receiving something, so *to* is appropriate. Choice *D* introduces unnecessary commas.

43. B: Choice *B* is the correct answer because it appropriately applies a comma after the opening word *Sadly*. This is because the author is introducing an idea or feeling, then transitioning into an elaborative explanation. *Sadly* is an aside, so there must be a comma afterwards to transition between thoughts and avoid a long-winded sentence. Choice *A* lacks the comma, so it is incorrect. Choice *C* incorrectly separates *that are attacked as lies* from the rest of the sentence, breaking its flow. Choice *D* still lacks the comma and incorrectly changes the two past tense verbs, *plagued* and *attacked*, into gerunds.

44. D: Choice *D* is the correct answer because the tense of *understanding* best applies to the context of the sentence. *Understanding* is also preceded by the modifier *an*. The combined *an understanding* forms

a compound noun that is the direct object and focus of the sentence. Choices *A* and *B* use *understand* as a verb, which doesn't complement the sentence. Choice *C* lacks the modifying *an*.

Practice Test #3

Questions 1–15 are based on the following passage:

The knowledge of an aircraft engineer is acquired through years of education, and special (1) <u>licenses are required</u>. Ideally, an individual will begin his or her preparation for the profession in high school (2) <u>by taking chemistry physics trigonometry and calculus.</u> Such curricula will aid in (3) <u>one's pursuit of a bachelor's degree</u> in aircraft engineering, which requires several physical and life sciences, mathematics, and design courses.

(4) <u>Some of universities provide internship or apprentice opportunities</u> for the students enrolled in aircraft engineer programs. A bachelor's in aircraft engineering is commonly accompanied by a master's degree in advanced engineering or business administration. Such advanced degrees enable an individual to position himself or herself for executive, faculty, and/or research opportunities. (5) <u>These advanced offices oftentimes require a Professional Engineering (PE) license which can be obtained through additional college courses, professional experience, and acceptable scores on the Fundamentals of Engineering (FE) and Professional Engineering (PE) standardized assessments.</u>

(6) <u>Once the job begins, this lines of work</u> requires critical thinking, business skills, problem solving, and creativity. This level of (7) <u>expertise</u> (8) <u>allows</u> aircraft engineers to (9) <u>apply mathematical equation and scientific processes</u> to aeronautical and aerospace issues or inventions. (10) <u>For example,</u> aircraft engineers may test, design, and construct flying vessels such as airplanes, space shuttles, and missile weapons. As a result, aircraft engineers are compensated with generous salaries. In fact, in May 2014, the lowest 10 percent of all American aircraft engineers earned less than $60,110 while the highest paid ten-percent of all American aircraft engineers earned $155,240. (11) <u>In May 2015, the United States Bureau of Labor Statistics (BLS) reported that the median annual salary of aircraft engineers was $107,830.</u> (12) <u>Conversely,</u> (13) <u>employment opportunities for aircraft engineers are projected to decrease by 2 percent by 2024.</u> This decrease may be the result of a decline in the manufacturing industry. (14) <u>Nevertheless aircraft engineers who know how to utilize</u> modeling and simulation programs, fluid dynamic software, and robotic engineering tools (15) <u>is projected to remain</u> the most employable.

1. Which of the following would be the best choice for this sentence (reproduced below)?

The knowledge of an aircraft engineer is acquired through years of education, and special (1) <u>licenses are required</u>.

a. NO CHANGE
b. licenses will be required
c. licenses may be required
d. licenses should be required

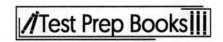

2. Which of the following would be the best choice for this sentence (reproduced below)?

Ideally, an individual will begin his or her preparation for the profession in high school (2) <u>by taking chemistry physics trigonometry and calculus.</u>

a. NO CHANGE
b. by taking chemistry; physics; trigonometry; and calculus.
c. by taking chemistry, physics, trigonometry, and calculus.
d. by taking chemistry, physics, trigonometry, calculus.

3. Which of the following would be the best choice for this sentence (reproduced below)?

Such curricula will aid in (3) <u>one's pursuit of a bachelor's degree</u> in aircraft engineering, which requires several physical and life sciences, mathematics, and design courses.

a. NO CHANGE
b. ones pursuit of a bachelors degree
c. one's pursuit of a bachelors degree
d. ones pursuit of a bachelor's degree

4. Which of the following would be the best choice for this sentence (reproduced below)?

(4) <u>Some of universities provide internship or apprentice opportunities</u> for the students enrolled in aircraft engineer programs.

a. NO CHANGE
b. Some of universities provided internship or apprentice opportunities
c. Some of universities provide internship or apprenticeship opportunities
d. Some universities provide internship or apprenticeship opportunities

5. Which of the following would be the best choice for this sentence (reproduced below)?

(5) <u>These advanced offices oftentimes require a Professional Engineering (PE) license which can be obtained through additional college courses, professional experience, and acceptable scores on the Fundamentals of Engineering (FE) and Professional Engineering (PE) standardized assessments.</u>

a. NO CHANGE
b. These advanced positions oftentimes require acceptable scores on the Fundamentals of Engineering (FE) and Professional Engineering (PE) standardized assessments in order to achieve a Professional Engineering (PE) license. Additional college courses and professional experience help.
c. These advanced offices oftentimes require acceptable scores on the Fundamentals of Engineering (FE) and Professional Engineering (PE) standardized assessments to gain the Professional Engineering (PE) license which can be obtained through additional college courses, professional experience.
d. These advanced positions oftentimes require a Professional Engineering (PE) license which is obtained by acceptable scores on the Fundamentals of Engineering (FE) and Professional Engineering (PE) standardized assessments. Further education and professional experience can help prepare for the assessments.

6. Which of the following would be the best choice for this sentence (reproduced below)?

   (6) <u>Once the job begins, this lines of work</u> requires critical thinking, business skills, problem solving, and creativity.

   a. NO CHANGE
   b. Once the job begins, this line of work
   c. Once the job begins, these line of work
   d. Once the job begin, this line of work

7. Which of the following would be the best choice for this sentence (reproduced below)?

   This level of (7) <u>expertise</u> allows aircraft engineers to apply mathematical equation and scientific processes to aeronautical and aerospace issues or inventions.

   a. NO CHANGE
   b. expertis
   c. expirtise
   d. excpertise

8. Which of the following would be the best choice for this sentence (reproduced below)?

   This level of expertise (8) <u>allows</u> aircraft engineers to apply mathematical equation and scientific processes to aeronautical and aerospace issues or inventions.

   a. NO CHANGE
   b. Inhibits
   c. Requires
   d. Should

9. Which of the following would be the best choice for this sentence (reproduced below)?

   This level of expertise allows aircraft engineers to (9) <u>apply mathematical equation and scientific processes</u> to aeronautical and aerospace issues or inventions.

   a. NO CHANGE
   b. apply mathematical equations and scientific process
   c. apply mathematical equation and scientific process
   d. apply mathematical equations and scientific processes

10. Which of the following would be the best choice for this sentence (reproduced below)?

    (10) <u>For example,</u> aircraft engineers may test, design, and construct flying vessels such as airplanes, space shuttles, and missile weapons.

    a. NO CHANGE
    b. Therefore,
    c. However,
    d. Furthermore,

11. Which of the following would be the best choice for this sentence (reproduced below)?

(11) In May of 2015, the United States Bureau of Labor Statistics (BLS) reported that the median annual salary of aircraft engineers was $107,830.

a. NO CHANGE
b. May of 2015, the United States Bureau of Labor Statistics (BLS) reported that the median annual salary of aircraft engineers was $107,830.
c. In May of 2015 the United States Bureau of Labor Statistics (BLS) reported that the median annual salary of aircraft engineers was $107,830.
d. In May, 2015, the United States Bureau of Labor Statistics (BLS) reported that the median annual salary of aircraft engineers was $107,830.

12. Which of the following would be the best choice for this sentence (reproduced below)?

(12) Conversely, employment opportunities for aircraft engineers are projected to decrease by 2 percent by 2024.

a. NO CHANGE
b. Similarly,
c. In other words,
d. Accordingly,

13. Which of the following would be the best choice for this sentence (reproduced below)?

Conversely, (13) employment opportunities for aircraft engineers are projected to decrease by 2 percent by 2024.

a. NO CHANGE
b. employment opportunities for aircraft engineers will be projected to decrease by 2 percent in 2024.
c. employment opportunities for aircraft engineers is projected to decrease by 2 percent in 2024.
d. employment opportunities for aircraft engineers was projected to decrease by 2 percent in 2024.

14. Which of the following would be the best choice for this sentence (reproduced below)?

(14) Nevertheless aircraft engineers who know how to utilize modeling and simulation programs, fluid dynamic software, and robotic engineering tools is projected to remain the most employable.

a. NO CHANGE
b. Nevertheless; aircraft engineers who know how to utilize
c. Nevertheless, aircraft engineers who know how to utilize
d. Nevertheless—aircraft engineers who know how to utilize

15. Which of the following would be the best choice for this sentence (reproduced below)?

Nevertheless aircraft engineers who know how to utilize modeling and simulation programs, fluid dynamic software, and robotic engineering tools (15) <u>is projected to remain</u> the most employable.

a. NO CHANGE
b. am projected to remain
c. was projected to remain
d. are projected to remain

Questions 16–30 are based on the following passage:

On September 11th, 2001, a group of terrorists hijacked four American airplanes. The terrorists crashed the planes into the World Trade Center in New York City, the Pentagon in Washington D.C., and a field in Pennsylvania. Nearly 3,000 people died during the attacks, which propelled the United States into a (16) <u>"War on Terror".</u>

About the Terrorists

(17) <u>Terrorists commonly uses fear and violence to achieve political goals.</u> The nineteen terrorists who orchestrated and implemented the attacks of September 11th were militants associated with al-Qaeda, an Islamic extremist group founded by Osama bin Laden, Abdullah Azzam, and others in the late 1980s. (18) <u>Bin Laden orchestrated the attacks as a response to what he felt was American injustice against Islam and hatred towards Muslims.</u> In his words, "Terrorism against America deserves to be praised."

Islam is the religion of Muslims, (19) <u>who live mainly in south and southwest Asia</u> and Sub-Saharan Africa. The majority of Muslims practice Islam peacefully. However, fractures in Islam have led to the growth of Islamic extremists who strictly oppose Western influences. They seek to institute stringent Islamic law and destroy those who violate Islamic code.

In November 2002, bin Laden provided the explicit motives for the 9/11 terror attacks. According to this list, (20) <u>Americas support of Israel,</u> military presence in Saudi Arabia, and other anti-Muslim actions were the causes.

The Timeline of the Attacks

The morning of September 11 began like any other for most Americans. Then, at 8:45 a.m., a Boeing 767 plane (21) <u>crashed into the north tower of the World Trade Center</u> in New York City. Hundreds were instantly killed. Others were trapped on higher floors. The crash was initially thought to be a freak accident. When a second plane flew directly into the south tower eighteen minutes later, it was determined that America was under attack.

At 9:45 a.m., (22) <u>slamming into the Pentagon was a third plane,</u> America's military headquarters in Washington D.C. The jet fuel of this plane caused a major fire and partial building collapse that resulted in nearly 200 deaths. By 10:00 a.m., the south tower of the World Trade Center collapsed. Thirty minutes later, the north tower followed suit.

While this was happening, a fourth plane that departed from New Jersey, United Flight 93, was hijacked. The passengers learned of the attacks that occurred in New York and Washington D.C. and realized that they faced the same fate as the other planes that crashed. The passengers were determined to overpower the terrorists in an effort to prevent the deaths of additional innocent American citizens. Although the passengers were successful in (23) <u>diverging</u> the plane, it crashed in a western Pennsylvania field and killed everyone on board. The plane's final target remains uncertain, (24) <u>but believed by many people was the fact that United Flight 93 was heading for the White House.</u>

Heroes and Rescuers

(25) <u>Close to 3,000 people died in the World Trade Center attacks.</u> This figure includes 343 New York City firefighters and paramedics, 23 New York City police officers, and 37 Port Authority officers. Nevertheless, thousands of men and women in service worked (26) <u>valiantly</u> to evacuate the buildings, save trapped workers, extinguish infernos, uncover victims trapped in fallen rubble, and tend to nearly 10,000 injured individuals.

About 300 rescue dogs played a major role in the after-attack salvages. Working twelve-hour shifts, the dogs scoured the rubble and alerted paramedics when they found signs of life. While doing so, the dogs served as a source of comfort and therapy for the rescue teams.

Initial Impacts on America

The attacks of September 11, 2001 resulted in the immediate suspension of all air travel. No flights could take off from or land on American soil. (27) <u>American airports and airspace closed to all national and international flights.</u> Therefore, over five hundred flights had to turn back or be redirected to other countries. Canada alone received 226 flights and thousands of stranded passengers. (28) <u>Needless to say, as cancelled flights are rescheduled, air travel became backed up and chaotic for quite some time.</u>

At the time of the attacks, George W. Bush was the president of the United States. President Bush announced that "We will make no distinction between the terrorists who committed these acts and those who harbor them." The rate of hate crimes against American Muslims spiked, despite President Bush's call for the country to treat them with respect.

Additionally, relief funds were quickly arranged. The funds were used to support families of the victims, orphaned children, and those with major injuries. In this way, the tragic event brought the citizens together through acts of service towards those directly impacted by the attack.

Long-Term Effects of the Attacks

Over the past fifteen years, the attacks of September 11th have transformed the United States' government, travel safety protocols, and international relations. Anti-terrorism legislation became a priority for many countries as law enforcement and intelligence agencies teamed up to find and defeat alleged terrorists.

Present George W. Bush announced a War on Terror. He (29) <u>desired</u> to bring bin Laden and al-Qaeda to justice and prevent future terrorist networks from gaining strength. The War in Afghanistan began in October of 2001 when the United States and British forces bombed al-Qaeda camps. (30) <u>The Taliban, a group of fundamental Muslims who protected Osama bin Laden, was overthrown on December 9, 2001. However, the war continued in order to defeat insurgency campaigns in neighboring countries.</u> Ten years later, the United State Navy SEALS killed Osama bin Laden in Pakistan. During 2014, the United States declared the end of its involvement in the War on Terror in Afghanistan.

Museums and memorials have since been erected to honor and remember the thousands of people who died during the September 11th attacks, including the brave rescue workers who gave their lives in the effort to help others.

16. Which of the following would be the best choice for this sentence (reproduced below)?

Nearly 3,000 people died during the attacks, which propelled the United States into a (16) <u>"War on Terror".</u>

a. NO CHANGE
b. "war on terror".
c. "war on terror."
d. "War on Terror."

17. Which of the following would be the best choice for this sentence (reproduced below)?

(17) <u>Terrorists commonly uses fear and violence to achieve political goals.</u>

a. NO CHANGE
b. Terrorist's commonly use fear and violence to achieve political goals.
c. Terrorists commonly use fear and violence to achieve political goals.
d. Terrorists commonly use fear and violence to achieves political goals.

18. Which of the following would be the best choice for this sentence (reproduced below)?

(18) <u>Bin Laden orchestrated the attacks as a response to what he felt was American injustice against Islam and hatred towards Muslims.</u>

a. NO CHANGE
b. Bin Laden orchestrated the attacks as a response to what he felt was American injustice against Islam, and hatred towards Muslims.
c. Bin Laden orchestrated the attacks, as a response to what he felt was American injustice against Islam and hatred towards Muslims.
d. Bin Laden orchestrated the attacks as responding to what he felt was American injustice against Islam and hatred towards Muslims.

19. Which of the following would be the best choice for this sentence (reproduced below)?

Islam is the religion of Muslims, (19) who live mainly in south and southwest Asia and Sub-Saharan Africa.

a. NO CHANGE
b. who live mainly in the South and Southwest Asia
c. who live mainly in the south and Southwest Asia
d. who live mainly in the south and southwest asia

20. Which of the following would be the best choice for this sentence (reproduced below)?

According to this list, (20) Americas support of Israel, military presence in Saudi Arabia, and other anti-Muslim actions were the causes.

a. NO CHANGE
b. America's support of israel,
c. Americas support of Israel
d. America's support of Israel,

21. Which of the following would be the best choice for this sentence (reproduced below)?

Then, at 8:45 a.m., a Boeing 767 plane (21) crashed into the north tower of the World Trade Center in New York City.

a. NO CHANGE
b. crashes into the north tower of the World Trade Center
c. crashing into the north tower of the World Trade Center
d. crash into the north tower of the World Trade Center

22. Which of the following would be the best choice for this sentence (reproduced below)?

At 9:45 a.m., (22) slamming into the Pentagon was a third plane, America's military headquarters in Washington D.C.

a. NO CHANGE
b. into the Pentagon slammed a third plane,
c. a third plane slammed into the Pentagon,
d. the Pentagon was slamming by a third plane,

23. Which of the following would be the best choice for this sentence (reproduced below)?

Although the passengers were successful in (23) diverging the plane, it crashed in a western Pennsylvania field and killed everyone on board.

a. NO CHANGE
b. Diverting
c. Converging
d. Distracting

24. Which of the following would be the best choice for this sentence (reproduced below)?

The plane's final target remains uncertain, (24) <u>but believed by many people was the fact that United Flight 93 was heading for the White House.</u>

a. NO CHANGE
b. but many believe that United Flight 93 was heading for the White House.
c. also heading for the white house United Flight 93 was believed to be.
d. then many believe that United Flight 93 was heading for the White House.

25. Which of the following would be the best choice for this sentence (reproduced below)?

(25) <u>Close to 3,000 people died in the World Trade Center attacks.</u>

a. NO CHANGE
b. 3,000 people in the World Trade Center attacks died.
c. Dying in the World Trade Center attacks were around 3,000 people.
d. In the World Trade Center attacks were around 3,000 people dying.

26. Which of the following would be the best choice for this sentence (reproduced below)?

Nevertheless, thousands of men and women in service worked (26) <u>valiantly</u> to evacuate the buildings, save trapped workers, extinguish infernos, uncover victims trapped in fallen rubble, and tend to nearly 10,000 injured individuals.

a. NO CHANGE
b. valiently
c. valently
d. vanlyantly

27. Which of the following would be the best choice for this sentence (reproduced below)?

(27) <u>American airports and airspace closed to all national and international flights.</u>

a. NO CHANGE
b. American airports and airspace close to all national and international flights.
c. American airports and airspaces closed to all national and international flights.
d. American airspace and airports were closed to all national and international flights.

28. Which of the following would be the best choice for this sentence (reproduced below)?

(28) <u>Needless to say, as cancelled flights are rescheduled, air travel became backed up and chaotic for quite some time.</u>

a. NO CHANGE
b. As cancelled flights are rescheduled, air travel became backed up and chaotic for quite some time.
c. Needless to say, as cancelled flights were rescheduled, air travel became backed up and chaotic for quite some time.
d. Needless to say, as cancelled flights are rescheduled, air travel became backed up and chaotic over a period of time.

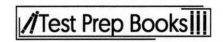

29. Which of the following would be the best choice for this sentence (reproduced below)?

He (29) <u>desired</u> to bring bin Laden and al-Qaeda to justice and prevent future terrorist networks from gaining strength.

a. NO CHANGE
b. Perceived
c. Intended
d. Assimilated

30. Which of the following would be the best choice for this sentence (reproduced below)?

(30) <u>The Taliban, a group of fundamental Muslims who protected Osama bin Laden, was overthrown on December 9, 2001. However, the war continued in order to defeat insurgency campaigns in neighboring countries.</u>

a. NO CHANGE
b. The Taliban was overthrown on December 9, 2001. They were a group of fundamental Muslims who protected Osama bin Laden. However, the war continued in order to defeat insurgency campaigns in neighboring countries.
c. The Taliban, a group of fundamental Muslims who protected Osama bin Laden, on December 9, 2001 was overthrown. However, the war continued in order to defeat insurgency campaigns in neighboring countries.
d. Osama bin Laden's fundamental Muslims who protected him were called the Taliban and overthrown on December 9, 2001. Yet the war continued in order to defeat the insurgency campaigns in neighboring countries.

Questions 31–46 are based on the following passage:

(31) <u>Seeing a lasting social change for African American people Fred Hampton desired to see</u> through nonviolent means and community recognition. (32) <u>As a result, he became an African American activist</u> during the American Civil Rights Movement and led the Chicago chapter of the Black Panther Party.

Hampton's Education

(33) <u>Born and raised in Maywood of Chicago, Illinois in 1948 was Hampton.</u> (34) <u>He was gifted academically and a natural athlete,</u> he became a stellar baseball player in high school. (35) <u>After graduating from Proviso East High School in 1966, he later went on to study law at Triton Junior College.</u>

While studying at Triton, Hampton joined and became a leader of the National Association for the Advancement of Colored People (NAACP). (36) <u>The NAACP gained more than 500 members resulting from his membership.</u> Hampton worked relentlessly to acquire recreational facilities in the neighborhood and improve the educational resources provided to the impoverished black community of Maywood.

The Black Panthers

The Black Panther Party (BPP) was another activist group that formed around the same time as the NAACP. Hampton was quickly attracted to the Black Panther's approach to the fight for equal rights for African Americans. (37) Hampton eventually joined the chapter, and relocated to downtown Chicago to be closer to its headquarters.

His charismatic personality, organizational abilities, sheer determination, and rhetorical skills enabled him to (38) quickly risen through the chapter's ranks. (39) Hampton soon became the leader of the Chicago chapter of the BPP where he organized rallies, taught political education classes, and established a free medical clinic. He also took part in the community police supervision project and played an instrumental role in the BPP breakfast program for impoverished African American children.

(40) Leading the BPP Hampton's greatest achievement may be his fight against street gang violence in Chicago. In 1969, (41) Hampton was held by a press conference where he made the gangs agree to a nonaggression pact known as the Rainbow Coalition. As a result of the pact, a multiracial alliance between blacks, Puerto Ricans, and poor youth was developed.

Assassination

As the Black Panther Party's popularity and influence grew, the Federal Bureau of Investigation (FBI) placed the group under constant surveillance. In an attempt to (42) neutralize the party, the FBI launched several harassment campaigns against the BPP, raided its headquarters in Chicago three times, and arrested over one hundred of the group's members. (43) During such a raid that occurred Hampton was shot on the morning of December 4th 1969.

In 1976, seven years after the event, it was revealed that William O'Neal, Hampton's trusted bodyguard, was an undercover FBI agent. (44) O'Neal provided the FBI with detailed floor plans of the BPP's headquarters, identifying the exact location of Hampton's bed. (45) It was because of these floor plans that the police were able to target and kill Hampton.

The assassination of Hampton fueled outrage amongst the African American community. It was not until years after the assassination that the police admitted wrongdoing. The Chicago City Council now (46) commemorates December 4th as Fred Hampton Day.

31. Which of the following would be the best choice for this sentence (reproduced below)?

(31) Seeing a lasting social change for African American people Fred Hampton desired to see through nonviolent means and community recognition.

a. NO CHANGE
b. Desiring to see a lasting social change for African American people, Fred Hampton
c. Fred Hampton desired to see lasting social change for African American people
d. Fred Hampton desiring to see last social change for African American people

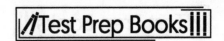

32. Which of the following would be the best choice for this sentence (reproduced below)?

(32) As a result, he became an African American activist during the American Civil Rights Movement and led the Chicago chapter of the Black Panther Party.

a. NO CHANGE
b. As a result he became an African American activist
c. As a result: he became an African American activist
d. As a result of, he became an African American activist

33. Which of the following would be the best choice for this sentence (reproduced below)?

(33) Born and raised in Maywood of Chicago, Illinois in 1948 was Hampton.

a. NO CHANGE
b. Hampton was born and raised in Maywood of Chicago, Illinois in 1948.
c. Hampton is born and raised in Maywood of Chicago, Illinois in 1948.
d. Hampton was born and raised in Maywood of Chicago Illinois in 1948.

34. Which of the following would be the best choice for this sentence (reproduced below)?

(34) He was gifted academically and a natural athlete, he became a stellar baseball player in high school.

a. NO CHANGE
b. A natural athlete and gifted though he was,
c. A natural athlete, and gifted,
d. Gifted academically and a natural athlete,

35. Which of the following would be the best choice for this sentence (reproduced below)?

(35) After graduating from Proviso East High School in 1966, he later went on to study law at Triton Junior College.

a. NO CHANGE
b. He later went on to study law at Triton Junior College graduating from Proviso East High School in 1966.
c. Graduating from Proviso East High School and Triton Junior College went to study.
d. Later at Triton Junior College, studying law, from Proviso East High School in 1966.

36. Which of the following would be the best choice for this sentence (reproduced below)?

(36) The NAACP gained more than 500 members resulting from his membership.

a. NO CHANGE
b. A gain of 500 members happened to the NAACP due to his membership.
c. As a result of his leadership, the NAACP gained more than 500 members.
d. 500 members were gained due to his NAACP membership.

37. Which of the following would be the best choice for this sentence (reproduced below)?

(37) Hampton eventually joined the chapter, and relocated to downtown Chicago to be closer to its headquarters.

a. NO CHANGE
b. Hampton eventually joined the chapter; and relocated to downtown Chicago to be closer to its headquarters.
c. Hampton eventually joined the chapter relocated to downtown Chicago to be closer to its headquarters.
d. Hampton eventually joined the chapter and relocated to downtown Chicago to be closer to its headquarters.

38. Which of the following would be the best choice for this sentence (reproduced below)?

His charismatic personality, organizational abilities, sheer determination, and rhetorical skills enabled him to (38) quickly risen through the chapter's ranks.

a. NO CHANGE
b. quickly rise
c. quickly rose
d. quickly rosed

39. Which of the following would be the best choice for this sentence (reproduced below)?

(39) Hampton soon became the leader of the Chicago chapter of the BPP where he organized rallies, taught political education classes, and established a free medical clinic.

a. NO CHANGE
b. As the leader of the BPP, Hampton: organized rallies, taught political education classes, and established a free medical clinic.
c. As the leader of the BPP, Hampton; organized rallies, taught political education classes, and established a free medical clinic.
d. As the leader of the BPP, Hampton—organized rallies, taught political education classes, and established a medical free clinic.

40. Which of the following would be the best choice for this sentence (reproduced below)?

(40) Leading the BPP Hampton's greatest achievement may be his fight against street gang violence in Chicago.

a. NO CHANGE
b. Greatest achievement of Hampton leading the BPP
c. Hampton's greatest achievement as the leader of the BPP
d. Leader of the BPP Hampton and greatest achievement

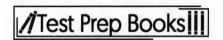

41. Which of the following would be the best choice for this sentence (reproduced below)?

    In 1969, (41) <u>Hampton was held by a press conference</u> where he made the gangs agree to a nonaggression pact known as the Rainbow Coalition.

    a. NO CHANGE
    b. a press conference held Hampton
    c. held by a press conference was Hampton
    d. Hampton held a press conference

42. Which of the following would be the best choice for this sentence (reproduced below)?

    In an attempt to (42) <u>neutralize</u> the party, the FBI launched several harassment campaigns against the BPP, raided its headquarters in Chicago three times, and arrested over one hundred of the group's members.

    a. NO CHANGE
    b. Accommodate
    c. Assuage
    d. Praise

43. Which of the following would be the best choice for this sentence (reproduced below)?

    (43) <u>During such a raid that occurred Hampton was shot</u> on the morning of December 4th 1969.

    a. NO CHANGE
    b. A raid, occurring because Hampton was shot
    c. Hampton was shot during such a raid that occurred
    d. Such a raid that occurred, Hampton was shot at

44. Which of the following would be the best choice for this sentence (reproduced below)?

    (44) <u>O'Neal provided the FBI with detailed</u> floor plans of the BPP's headquarters, identifying the exact location of Hampton's bed.

    a. NO CHANGE
    b. O'Neal is providing
    c. O'Neal provides
    d. O'Neal provided

Answer Explanations #3

1. C: The next paragraph states that "These advanced offices oftentimes require a Professional Engineering (PE) license which can be obtained through additional college courses, professional experience, and acceptable scores on the Fundamentals of Engineering (FE) and Professional Engineering (PE) standardized assessments." Since the word *oftentimes* is used instead of *always*, Choice *C* is the best response.

2. C: The best answer is Choice *C*. Items in a list should be separated by a comma. Choice *A* is incorrect because there are no commas within the list to separate the items. Choice *B* is incorrect; a semicolon is used in a series only when a comma is present within the list itself. Choice *D* is incorrect because the conjunction *and* is missing before the word *calculus*.

3. A: The sentence is correct as-is. The words *one* and *bachelor* have apostrophe -*s* at the end because they show possession for the words that come after. The other answer choices do not indicate possession is being shown.

4. D: To begin, *of* is not required here. *Apprenticeship* is also more appropriate in this context than *apprentice opportunities*; *apprentice* describes an individual in an apprenticeship, not an apprenticeship itself. Both of these changes are needed, making Choice *D* the correct answer.

5. D: Choice *D* is correct because it breaks the section into coherent sentences and emphasizes the main point the author is trying to communicate: the PE license is required for some higher positions, it's obtained by scoring well on the two standardized assessments, and college and experience can be used to prepare for the assessments in order to gain the certification. The original sentence is a run-on and contains confusing information, so Choice *A* is incorrect. Choice *B* fixes the run-on aspect, but the sentence is indirect and awkward in construction. Choice *C* is incorrect for the same reason as Choice *B*, and it is a run on.

6. B: *Once the job begins, this line of work* is the best way to phrase this sentence. Choice *A* is incorrect because *lines* does not match up with *this*; it would instead match up with the word *these*. Choice *C* is incorrect; *these line* should say *this line*. Choice *D* is incorrect; *job begin* is faulty subject/verb agreement.

7. A: The word is spelled correctly as it is: *expertise*.

8. C: *Allows* is inappropriate because it does not stress what those in the position of aircraft engineers actually need to be able to do. *Requires* is the only alternative that fits because it actually describes necessary skills of the job.

9. D: The words *equations* and *processes* in this sentence should be plural. Choices *A, B,* and *C* have one or both words as singular, which is incorrect.

10. A: The correct response is Choice *A* because this statement's intent is to give examples as to how aircraft engineers apply mathematical equations and scientific processes towards aeronautical and aerospace issues and/or inventions. The answer is not *Therefore*, Choice *B*, or *Furthermore*, Choice *D*, because no causality is being made between ideas. Two items are neither being compared nor contrasted, so *However*, Choice *C*, is also not the correct answer.

11. A: No change is required. The comma is properly placed after the introductory phrase *In May of 2015.* Choice *B* is missing the word *In.* Choice *C* does not separate the introductory phrase from the rest of the sentence. Choice *D* places an extra comma prior to 2015.

12. A: The word *conversely* best demonstrates the opposite sentiments in this passage. Choice *B* is incorrect because it denotes agreement with the previous statement. Choice *C* is incorrect because the sentiment is not restated but opposed. Choice *D* is incorrect because the previous statement is not a cause for the sentence in question.

13. A: The correct answer is Choice *A, are projected.* The present tense *are* matches with the rest of the sentence. The verb *are* also matches with the plural *employment opportunities.* Choice *B* uses *will be projected,* which is incorrect because the statistic is being used as evidence, which demands a present or past tense verb. In this case it is present tense to maintain consistency. Choice *C* is incorrect because the singular verb *is* does not match with the plural subject *employment opportunities.* Choice *D* is incorrect because the past tense verb *were* does not maintain consistency with the present tense in the rest of the passage.

14. C: Choice *C* is the best answer because introductory words like "Nevertheless" are always succeeded by a comma.

15. D: The main subject and verb in this sentence are far apart from each other. The subject is *engineers* and the subject is *are projected.* Although there is a clause which interrupts the subject and the verb, they still must agree with each other.

16. D: The correct phrase should be "War on Terror." The phrase is capitalized because it was part of the campaign phrase that was launched by the U.S. government after September 11. Punctuation should always be used inside double quotes as well, making Choice *D* the best answer.

17. C: Terrorists commonly use fear and violence to achieve political goals. Choice *A* is incorrect because the subject *Terrorists* is plural while the verb *uses* is singular, so the subject and verb do not agree with each other. Choice *B* is incorrect because the word *Terrorist's* with the apostrophe *-s* shows possession, but the terrorists aren't in possession of anything in this sentence. Choice *D* is incorrect because the word *achieves* should be *achieve.*

18. A: No change is needed. Choices *B* and *C* utilize incorrect comma placements. Choice *D* utilizes an incorrect verb tense (*responding*).

19. B: The best answer Choice is *B, who live mainly in the South and Southwest Asia.* The directional terms *South Asia* and *Southwest Asia* are integral parts of a proper name and should therefore be capitalized.

20. D: This is the best answer choice because *America's* with the apostrophe *-s* shows possession of the word *support,* and *Israel* should be capitalized because it is a country and therefore a proper noun. Choice *A* does not show possession in the word *Americas.* Choice *B* does not capitalize the word *Israel.* Choice *C* does not show possession and does not include the necessary comma at the end of the phrase.

21. A: This sentence is correct as-is. The verb tense should be in the past—the other three answer choices either have a present or continuous verb tense, so these are incorrect.

22. C: Choice *C* is the most straightforward version of this independent clause, because follows the "subject + verb + prepositional phrase" order which usually provides the most clarity.

23. B: Although *diverging* means to separate from the main route and go in a different direction, it is used awkwardly and unconventionally in this sentence. Therefore, Choice *A* is not the answer. Choice *B* is the correct answer because it implies that the passengers distracted the terrorists, which caused a change in the plane's direction. *Converging*, Choice *C,* is incorrect because it implies that the plane met another in a central location. Although the passengers may have distracted the terrorists, they did not distract the plane. Therefore, Choice *D* is incorrect.

24. B: Choice *B* is the best answer because it is straightforward and clear. Choice *A* is incorrect because the phrase *the fact that* is redundant. Choice *C* is inverted and doesn't make much sense because the subject comes after the verb. Choice *D* is incorrect because it does not have the appropriate transition, *but*, which is intended to show a contrast to the *uncertainty* phrase that comes before it.

25. A: Choice *A* is the best choice for this sentence because it is the most straightforward and easiest to understand. Choice *B* is incorrect because it leaves out the hedging language. Choice *C* keeps the hedging language, but the sentence begins with a verb which is not the best decision for clarity. Choice *D* is incorrect because it begins with a preposition which is not the best choice for a straightforward presentation of the facts.

26. A: The word *valiantly* is spelled correctly in the original sentence.

27. D: Airspace and airports must be closed by people; they don't just close themselves, so it is proper to include an action to indicate that they were sealed off. Choice *B* is incorrect because the verb *close* is in the incorrect tense. Choice *C* is also incorrect because *airspace* does not need to become *airspaces* and the issue still remains: while there is action, it is not in the proper form to indicate human action. Choice *D* is correct because it correctly uses the helping verb *were*, which indicates human action.

28. C: This sentence contains improper verb agreement in the fragment *as cancelled flights are rescheduled*. *Are* is a present-tense verb while *rescheduled* is a past-tense verb. Because the attacks occurred in the past, both verbs need to be written in the past tense, as done in Choice *C*.

29. C: *Intended* means planned or meant to. *Intended* is a far better choice than *desired,* because it would communicate goals and strategy more than simply saying that Bush desired to do something. *Desired* communicates wishing or direct motive. Choices *B* and *D* have irrelevant meanings and wouldn't serve the sentence at all.

30. A: The original structure of the two sentences is correct. Choice *B* lacks the direct nature that the original sentence has. By breaking up the sentences, the connection between the Taliban's defeat and the ongoing war is separated by an unnecessary second sentence. Choice *C* corrects this problem, but the fluidity of the sentence is marred because of the awkward construction of the first sentence. Choice *D* begins well but lacks the use of *was* before *overthrown*.

31. C: Choice *C* is the best answer choice here because we have "subject + verb + prepositional phrases" which is usually the most direct sentence combination. Choice *A* is incorrect because the verbs *seeing* and *see* are repetitive. Choice *B* is incorrect because the subject and verb are separated, which is not the best way to divulge information in this particular sentence. Choice *D* is incorrect because the sentence uses a continuous verb form instead of past tense.

32. A: The comma after *result* is necessary for the sentence structure, making it an imperative component. The original sentence is correct, making Choice *A* correct. Choice *B* is incorrect because it lacks the crucial comma that introduces a new idea. Choice *C* is incorrect because a colon is

unnecessary, and Choice *D* is incorrect because the addition of the word *of* is unnecessary when applied to the rest of the sentence.

33. B: Hampton was born and raised in Maywood of Chicago, Illinois in 1948. Choice *A* is incorrect because the subject and verb are at the end, and this is not the most straightforward syntax. Choice *C* is incorrect because the rest of the passage is in past tense. Choice *D* is incorrect because there should be a comma between the names of a city and a state.

34. D: Choice *D* is the best answer because it fixes the comma splice in the original sentence by creating a modifying clause at the beginning of the sentence. Choice *A* is incorrect because it contains a comma splice. Choice *B* is too wordy. Choice *C* has an unnecessary comma.

35. A: The sentence is correct as-is. Choice *B* is incorrect because we are missing the chronological signpost *after*. Choice *C* is incorrect because there is no subject represented in this sentence. Choice *D* is incorrect because it also doesn't have a subject.

36. C: Choice *C* is the best sentence because it is a compound sentence with the appropriate syntax. Choice *A* is incorrect because *resulting* is not as clear as the phrase *as a result*. Choice *B* is incorrect because the syntax is clunky—to say something happened to the NAACP rather than the NAACP making the gain is awkward. Choice *D* is incorrect because this is passive voice; active voice would be better to use here as in Choice *C.*

37. D: Choice *D* is the best answer. Choice *A* is incorrect; if the second clause was independent we would need a comma in the middle, but the two clauses have the same single subject, so a comma is unnecessary. Choice *B* is incorrect; semicolons go in between two independent clauses without conjunctions. Choice *C* is incorrect; there needs to be a conjunction before the word *relocated*.

38. B: *enabled him to quickly rise* is the best answer. Although the passage is in past tense, the verb *enabled* is followed by the "to + infinitive." The infinitive is the base form of the verb; that's why *rise* is the best answer choice, because the verb follows *to* and represents the infinitive after the verb *enabled.*

39. A: No change is needed. The list of events should be separated by a comma. Choice *B* is incorrect. Although a colon can be used to introduce a list of items, it is not a conventional choice for separating items within a series. Semicolons are used to separate at least three items in a series that have an internal comma. Therefore, Choice *C* is incorrect. Choice *D* is incorrect because a dash is not a conventional choice for punctuating items in a series.

40. C: *Hampton's greatest achievement as the leader of the BPP* is the best way to phrase this sentence because it is the most straightforward and clear. Choice *A* is incorrect because the sentence starts out with a gerund when it could start out with Hampton, reducing confusion as to who is leading the BPP. Choice *B* is incorrect for the same reason; the sentence starts off with the subject inside the preposition, which is not the best syntax. Choice *D* is incorrect because it doesn't signify that the achievement was Hampton's.

41. D: Choice *D* is the most straightforward answer, "Hampton held a press conference." Choice *A* is incorrect because usually one isn't held "by" a press conference. Choice *B* is incorrect because likewise, a press conference doesn't "hold" someone, but someone would "hold" a press conference. Choice *C* is incorrect because again, someone isn't held "by" a press conference, and the syntax is inverted here.

42. A: The term *neutralize* means to counteract, or render ineffective, which is exactly what the FBI is wanting to do. Accommodate means to be helpful or lend aid, which is the opposite of *neutralize*. Therefore, Choice *B* is incorrect. *Assuage* means to ease, while *praise* means to express warm feeling, so they are in no way close to the needed context. Therefore, *neutralize* is the best option, making Choice *A* the correct answer.

43. C: Choice *C* is the most straightforward answer choice. Choice *A* is incorrect because the sentence is inverted and not very clear. Choice *B* is incorrect because the change in syntax changes the meaning in the sentence. Choice *D* isn't the best way to organize the sentence because it creates wordiness.

44. D: Choice *D* is the best answer choice because it matches with the past tense of the passage. The other answer choices are either in present tense or a present continuous tense.

Dear SAT Test Taker,

We would like to start by thanking you for purchasing this study guide for your SAT exam. We hope that we exceeded your expectations.

Our goal in creating this study guide was to cover all of the topics that you will see on the test. We also strove to make our practice questions as similar as possible to what you will encounter on test day. With that being said, if you found something that you feel was not up to your standards, please send us an email and let us know.

We would also like to let you know about other books in our catalog that may interest you.

ACT

This can be found on Amazon: amazon.com/dp/1628454709

SAT Math 1

amazon.com/dp/1628458631

ACCUPLACER

amazon.com/dp/1628459344

TSI

amazon.com/dp/162845699X

AP Biology

amazon.com/dp/1628456221

We have study guides in a wide variety of fields. If the one you are looking for isn't listed above, then try searching for it on Amazon or send us an email.

Thanks Again and Happy Testing!

Product Development Team

info@studyguideteam.com

Interested in buying more than 10 copies of our product? Contact us about bulk discounts:

bulkorders@studyguideteam.com

FREE Test Taking Tips DVD Offer

To help us better serve you, we have developed a Test Taking Tips DVD that we would like to give you for FREE. **This DVD covers world-class test taking tips that you can use to be even more successful when you are taking your test.**

All that we ask is that you email us your feedback about your study guide. Please let us know what you thought about it – whether that is good, bad or indifferent.

To get your **FREE Test Taking Tips DVD**, email freedvd@studyguideteam.com with "FREE DVD" in the subject line and the following information in the body of the email:

    a. The title of your study guide.

    b. Your product rating on a scale of 1-5, with 5 being the highest rating.

    c. Your feedback about the study guide. What did you think of it?

    d. Your full name and shipping address to send your free DVD.

If you have any questions or concerns, please don't hesitate to contact us at freedvd@studyguideteam.com.

Thanks again!

9 781628 458151